NC   2.50

THE
FUNGUS-GROWING ANTS
OF NORTH AMERICA

THE
FUNGUS-GROWING ANTS
OF NORTH AMERICA

by
William Morton Wheeler

Dover Publications, Inc.
New York

Published in Canada by General Publishing Company, Ltd., 30 Lesmill Road, Don Mills, Toronto, Ontario.

Published in the United Kingdom by Constable and Company, Ltd., 10 Orange Street, London WC 2.

This Dover edition, first published in 1973, is an unabridged republication of the work that originally appeared as Article XXXI, pp. 669-807 of the *Bulletin of the American Museum of Natural History*, Vol. XXIII, published in New York, by order of the Trustees, 1907. The publisher gratefully acknowledges the cooperation of the University of Vermont Library, which lent a copy of this work for reproduction.

A new, detailed Table of Contents has been added to this edition.

International Standard Book Number: 0-486-21164-9
Library of Congress Catalog Card Number: 73-83351

Manufactured in the United States of America
Dover Publications, Inc.
180 Varick Street
New York, N. Y. 10014

PUBLISHER'S NOTE

The Fungus-growing Ants of North America originally appeared as Article XXXI, pp. 669-807, of the *Bulletin of the American Museum of Natural History,* Vol. XXIII, 1907. In the present edition the original page numbers [in square brackets] appear alongside the new numbers. The plates, found at the end of the monograph, retain their original numbers.

CONTENTS

viii   *Contents*

LIST OF ILLUSTRATIONS.

Introduction.

Among the multitudinous activities of insects, none are more marvellous than the fungus-growing and fungus-eating habits of the Attiine ants. Not only are these habits of interest as a most unusual specialization in diet — for all ants were originally and many are still exclusively entomophagous — but the successful cultivation of such delicate plants as fungi presupposes an astonishing range and complexity of adaptation even for these very plastic insects. This statement will be endorsed by those who have tried to obtain pure cultures of fungi either in the hot-house or the laboratory. Besides the selection of proper culture media and the accurate regulation of temperature and moisture, exquisite precautions have to be taken to exclude the germs of alien species. The Attii are able to achieve all this and, what is equally remarkable, at least two other groups of insects, namely, certain Old World termites and the "ambrosia beetles" (Tomicine Scolytidæ) of both hemispheres, have independently developed analogous habits.

The fungus-growing ants all belong to a single Myrmicine tribe, the Attii, and all the species of this tribe are fungus-growers. They are, moreover, confined almost exclusively to tropical and subtropical America, only a single species being known to range as far north as New Jersey. And since a few others occur as far south as Argentina, we may say that the geographical distribution of the tribe extends from 40° north to 40° south of the equator. About one hundred species, subspecies and varieties of Attii have been described and have been distributed among various genera and subgenera, as follows:

Genus *Atta* Fabricius.

Subgenus *Atta* sensu stricto, including: *A. cephalotes* L. with the vars. *lutea* Forel, *opaca* Forel, *polita* Emery and *integrior* Forel; *sexdens* L., with the subsp. *vollenweideri* Forel; *lævigata* F. Smith; *columbica* Guérin; *insularis* Guérin; *fervens* Drury; *texana* Buckley.

Subgenus *Mœllerius* Forel, including: *M. heyeri* Forel; *striata* Roger;

silvestrii Emery; *balzani* Emery; *landolti* Forel; *versicolor* Pergande with the subsp. *chisosensis* Wheeler.

Subgenus *Acromyrmex* Mayr, including: *A. subterranea* Forel; *lobicornis* Emery and its var. *ferruginea* Emery; *lundi* Guérin; *ambigua* Emery; *pubescens* Emery with the subsp. *bonariensis* Emery and *decolor* Emery; *emilii* Forel; *octospinosa* Reich with the var. *echinatior* Forel; *mœlleri* Forel with the vars. *panamensis* Forel and *meinerti* Forel, and the subsp. *modesta* Forel with the var. *andicola* Forel; *coronata* Forel; *mesonotalis* Emery; *discigera* Mayr; *muticinoda* Forel with the var. *homalops* Emery; *nigra* F. Smith; *aspersa* F. Smith with the var. *rugosa* F. Smith; *laticeps* Emery; *boliviensis* Emery; *iheringi* Emery.

Subgenus *Trachymyrmex* Forel, including: *T. urichi* Forel with the subsp. *fusca* Emery; *pruinosa* Emery; *septentrionalis* McCook with the var. *obscurior* Wheeler; *turrifex* Wheeler; *arizonensis* Wheeler; *jamaicensis* Ern. André; *saussurei* Forel; *squamulifera* Emery; *farinosa* Emery.

Subgenus *Mycetosoritis* Wheeler, including: *M. hartmanni* Wheeler; *aspera* Mayr.

Subgenus *Mycocepurus* Forel, including: *M. göldii* Forel, *smithi* Forel with the vars. *tolteca* Wheeler and *borinquenensis* Wheeler.

Genus *Cyphomyrmex* Mayr.

C. rimosus Spinola with the subsp. *minutus* Mayr, *salvini* Forel, *dentatus* Forel, *transversus* Emery and *olindanus* Forel, and the vars. *major* Forel, *fusca* Emery and *comalensis* Wheeler; *parallelus* Emery; *olitor* Forel; *auritus* Mayr; *morschi* Emery; *simplex* Emery; *strigatus* Mayr; *wheeleri* Forel; *kirbyi* Mayr; *flavidus* Pergande; *championi* Forel; *foxi* Ern. André; *bigibbosus* Emery.

Genus *Myrmicocrypta* F. Smith.

M. squamosa F. Smith; *dilacerta* Forel with the subsp. *cornuta* Forel; *subnitida* Forel; *godmani* Forel; *brittoni* Wheeler.

Genus *Sericomyrmex* Mayr.

S. opacus Mayr; *aztecus* Forel; *saussurei* Emery.

Genus *Apterostigma* Mayr.

A. pilosum Mayr; *scutellare* Forel; *mœlleri* Forel; *wasmanni* Forel; *urichi* Forel; *mayri* Forel; *collare* Emery; *robustum* Emery.

The various subgenera included under *Atta* sensu lato will probably be raised eventually to generic rank. The subgenus *Atta* comprises the leaf-cutting or parasol ants, the largest and most powerful species of the tribe, living in great colonies and inhabiting the territory between 30° north and 30° south of the equator. The workers are highly polymorphic and much smaller than the males and females. The colonies of the species of *Mœllerius* and *Acromyrmex* are much less populous, and the workers, though variable in size, do not exhibit such marked polymorphism as those of *Atta* s. str. In *Trachymyrmex* and the remaining subgenera the workers are monomorphic and but little smaller than the males and females, and the colonies are even feebler than those of *Acromyrmex*. *Mycetosoritis* and *Mycocepurus* are in certain respects transitional to the genera *Cyphomyrmex* and *Myrmicocrypta*, and species of the last show affinities with *Sericomyrmex*. *Apterostigma* is very aberrant, resembling in form certain Myrmicines of the subgenera *Aphænogaster* and *Ischnomyrmex*. The workers of *Atta* are covered with stiff, erect or suberect, hooked or curved hairs, and the surface of the body is tuberculate or spinose. In *Cyphomyrmex* the body is smoother and covered with short, appressed, scale-like hairs. In *Sericomyrmex* and *Apterostigma* the hairs are soft, flexuous and very abundant. With few exceptions all the Attii have the surface of the body opaque and of a ferruginous, brown or blackish color. All the species, moreover, though very powerful and able to make surprisingly extensive excavations in the soil, are very slow and stolid in their movements. The sting of the workers is vestigial, but in the larger species the sharp jaws may be used as most efficient organs of defence. The smaller species are extremely timid and when roughly handled "feign death" like Curculionid beetles. In all the species the hard, rough or spinose integument must afford efficient protection from alien ants and other enemies.

Owing to the labors of Forel, Emery and Mayr our knowledge of the taxonomy of the Attii is probably as satisfactory as that of any other groups of exotic ants. As much cannot, however, be said of our knowledge of the habits. Since all the Attii live in intimate symbiosis with fungi, a complete study of the habits of these insects requires the diligent coöperation of the entomologist and botanist. Hitherto the botanists, notably Alfred Mœller and Jakob Huber, have contributed the most accurate observations. As neither the botanists nor the entomologists of North America have shown any very serious interest in the Attii, I need not apologize for publishing the following pages.   Though these contribute little towards a solution of many of the outstanding problems, they nevertheless contain a number of observations that may be of permanent interest and value.   My attention was first attracted to these insects several years ago while I was sojourning in Texas. It was, in fact, the sight of a leaf-bearing file of *Atta texana*, moving along the bank of Barton Creek near Austin, one sultry afternoon in September, that first kindled my interest in the habits of ants.   I postponed publishing my notes on this and other species, hoping to have an opportunity to study a greater number of forms in the heart of the tropics, but as there is no immediate prospect of my being able to continue the work in these regions, I have decided to publish my observations as they stand.   The present article is divided into four parts, namely, a résumé of the writings of previous students of the Attii, a taxonomic revision of the known North American members of the group, including a few from Mexico and the West Indies, an account of my own observations on these same forms, and a general consideration of some of the main problems involved in the study of the fungus-growing instincts not only in the Attii but also in the termites and ambrosia beetles.

PART I.   HISTORICAL.

The large leaf-cutting ants of the genus *Atta* s. str. are such conspicuous, widely distributed, and destructive insects in tropical America that they must have been only too familiar to the indigenes and the early settlers in those regions.   That these ants figured prominently in the Indian mythologies is indicated by a passage in the Popul Vuh, a collection of Guatemalan traditions to which my friend Mr. F. Bandelier has called my attention.[1] This collection was made by Dominican friars, probably during the middle or latter half of the sixteenth century.   The following myth refers to the larger species of *Atta* which are known to collect the petals and whole flowers as well as the leaves of plants.   The mythical young men, Hunahpu and Xbalanqué, had been taken in ambush and required by their captors, Hun-Camé and Vukub-Camé to fetch four vases of certain flowers as a test, and to forfeit their lives in case of failure.   "Thus they stayed in the House of the Lances during the night, when they called on all the ants: "Cutting ants and zampopos,[2] come and together fetch the flowers designated by the princes."

---

[1] Popul Vuh. Livre Sacré et les Mythes de l' Antiquité Americaine avec les Livres Héroiques et Historiques des Quichés, par L' Abbé Brasseur de Bourbour.   Paris, Aug. Durand, 1861.

[2] *Zanic* is the generic name of the ant.   *Chequen-zanic* is a large ant which goes about at night cutting the stems of vegetables and tender flowers, as if with scissors.   Its name among the Hispano-Guatemalan peoples is *zampopo*.   (Commentator's note.)

"Very well," they replied.   Then all the ants set out to fetch the flowers of the garden of Hun-Camé and Vukub-Camé.   These had apprised the guardians of the flowers of Xibalba in advance: "As to you, give heed to our flowers; do not let these two young men, whom we have taken in ambush, carry off any of them.   Where else could they go to get those we have designated?   There are none elsewhere.   Watch closely therefore throughout the night."— "It is well," they replied.

"But the sentinels of the garden heard nothing of what was going on. In vain they went about, walking on their legs, among the branches of the trees of the garden, and repeating the same song.   "Xpurpurek, Xpurpurek! sang one.— "Puhuyu, puhuyu!" repeated the other.

"Puhuyu was the name of the two sentinels of the plantations of Hun-Camé and Vukub-Camé.   But they did not notice the ants stealing away what had been committed to their charge, going and coming in innumerable hordes, cutting down the flower beds, moving along with the flowers which they bore away in their jaws above the trees, while under the trees the flowers exhaled a sweet odor.

"Meanwhile the sentinels kept shouting with all their might, without noticing the teeth that were sawing at their tails and wings.[1]   There was a harvest of flowers mown down by their jaws and borne all odoriferous by their jaws into the House of the Lances.

"Very soon the four vases were filled with flowers, and they were quite full when the day dawned.   Soon thereafter the messengers came to seek them.   "Let them come," said the King, "and let them bring forthwith what we have demanded," said they to the young men.

"Very well," said they.   Thereupon they proceeded to fetch the four vases of flowers.   Then, having presented themselves before the king and the princes, these took the flowers whose sight it was a pleasure (to behold). Thus were those of Xibalba tricked.

"It was the ants alone who had been dispatched by the young men, and who in a single night had carried away all the flowers and placed them in the vases.   At this sight all the (princes) of Xibalba changed color and their faces paled on account of the flowers.

"Then they sent the men to seek the guardians of the flowers: "Why did you permit our flowers to be stolen.   Are these not our own flowers which we here behold?" said they to the guardians.— "We did not notice anything, my lord.   They did not even spare our tails," they replied.   Then they split the lips of the guardians, to punish them for having permitted the theft of that which was committed to their charge.

---

[1] The commentator states that he is unable to understand this allusion.   The guardians are evidently conceived as birds, as shown by the above reference to their "walking on their legs," although this is not clearly stated till the end of the passage.

"It was in this manner that Hun-Camé and Vukub-Camé were vanquished by Hunahpu and Xbalanqué, and this was the beginning of their labors. Thenceforth, too, the Purpueks had their mouths cleft, and cleft they are to this day." [1]

I am also indebted to Mr. Bandelier for the following extracts from the early historians of the Conquest. Gonzalo Fernandez de Oviedo y Valdes in his 'Historia de las Indias' (1535) gives an account of the pernicious ants and termites of Española (Santo Domingo). Among the former are certain species "which do very great damage throughout the island, in the plantations, destroying and burning up the cane and oranges and other useful plants." These ants must have been the large species of *Atta*, probably *A. insularis*, which does great damage to plantations also in the adjacent island of Cuba.

P. Bernabè Cobo, in his 'Historia de Neuvo Mundo' (1653) also describes a number of noxious ants in Santo Domingo. He says: "There is another kind of large ants which the Chiriquan Indians call Iczau, and it is these which eat the trees and whose young, when newly hatched, are called Icza, and are eaten by the Indians." These Iczau are evidently the virgin females of *Atta*. They are a so eaten by the Brazilian Indians who call them Iças, according to von Ihering (1894). Cobo seems to be the first author to record the use of the heads of *Atta* soldiers by the Indians for surgical purposes: "They use a certain species of the said ants, because they bite severely, for closing wounds instead of stitching them with a needle. This is done in the following manner: they bring together the skin of the two sides of the wound and apply these ants, which bite and hold the two sides or lips together and then they cut off the insects' heads, which remain attached to the wound with their mouths or mandibles as firmly closed as they were in life."

Specimens of the large *Attæ* were, of course, taken to Europe by the early travelers. Seba (1734–35) gives a good figure of a soldier of *A. cephalotes* or *sexdens* which found its way into his collection. Linné described both of these species, and they were also known to Fabricius and Latreille. The latter authors, apparently misled by the accounts of Mlle. Merian (1771), confounded the habits of these ants with those of the "fourmis de visites," or *Ecitons*.

The first naturalist to publish observations on any of the North American Attii was Buckley (1860), who studied the habits of *Atta texana* at Austin, Texas. He was evidently under the impression that this ant eats the leaves, berries, etc., which it carries into its nests. He unearthed some of the nests and describes the "soft grey spongy substance, apparently leaves, finely triturated and mixed with an animal secretion," found in the chambers. This "animal secretion" was undoubtedly the web of fungus hyphæ which binds the leaf particles together.

Bates (1863) in his classical 'Naturalist on the Amazon' gives an excellent account of *Atta cephalotes*, one of the ants called "Saubas" by the Brazilians. He described the extensive earthworks of this species, "large mounds of earth of a different color from the surrounding soil, which were thrown up in the plantations and woods. Some of these were very extensive, being forty yards in circumference, but not more than two feet in height..... The difference in color from the superficial soil of the vicinity is owing to their being formed of the subsoil, brought up from a considerable depth." He describes the manner in which the ants cut out pieces of leaves and the ensuing damage to cultivated trees and shrubs, and believes that "the leaves are used to thatch the domes which cover the entrances to their subterranean dwellings, thereby protecting from the deluging rains the young broods in the nests beneath." This erroneous inference was derived from seeing the workers "troop up" and cast their pieces of leaves on the hillocks of the nest where some of them are often covered by the earth brought up by the excavating workers. Bates also records the following observation to show the extent of the subterranean burrows of the Sauba: "The Rev. Hamlet Clark has related that the Saüba of Rio de Janeiro, a species closely allied to ours, has excavated a tunnel under the bed of the river Parahyba, at a place where it is as broad as the Thames at London Bridge. At the Magaory rice mills, near Para, these ants once pierced the embankment of a large reservoir: the great body of water which it contained escaped before the damage could be repaired. In the Botanic Gardens at Para, an enterprising French gardener tried all he could think of to extirpate the saüba. With this object he made fires over some of the main entrances to their colonies and blew the fumes of sulphur down the galleries by means of bellows. I saw the smoke issue from a great number of outlets, one of which was 70 yards distant from the place where the bellows were used." This ant not only does great damage to the foliage but also plunders stores of vegetable provisions such as farina or mandioca meal in houses at night. Bates observed the division of labor among the castes although he did not accurately define the soldier, or worker major. From the fact that the latter are often seen to be simply stalking about, he concluded that their "enormously large, hard and indestructible heads may be of use in protecting them against the attacks of insectivorous animals. They would be, in this view, a kind of 'pièces de resistance,' serving as a foil against onslaughts made on the main body of workers." Had Bates undertaken to excavate a large colony of these ants he would soon have discovered that these soldiers have a very important function to perform in the active defence of their fellow ants.

Lincecum in 1867 recorded a number of observations on *Atta texana* which, like his other publications on ants, are a strange jumble of truth and fiction. He states rather positively that this ant eats the vegetable substances which it collects. "In my observations on the habits of the cutting ants, I have not discovered them eating anything besides the foliage of various plants. Neither have I ever noticed them carrying anything else into their cities. Professor S. B. Buckley, who is a very close and accurate observer [sic!] states that he saw them carrying hackberries (*Celtis occidentalis*) and that they eat insects, tumble bugs, etc....From the immense quantities of leaves collected by them during the autumnal months, which are carefully sun-dried and taken into the city, I should feel at a loss to say, if they are not intended for winter food, what other use they can put such quantities of leaves to; and furthermore, when it is known to be the kind of food upon which they subsist." It is interesting to note that while Lincecum overlooked the marvellous fungus-raising habits of *Atta texana* he nevertheless attributed to them certain horticultural interests: "The cutting-ants plant seeds of various trees, vines and other plants. When they locate a city in a bald prairie, which is often the case, where they cannot procure the seeds of trees, they cultivate the prickly poppy (*Argemone Mexicana*) the most appropriate plant for their purpose that grows in the prairie.... When the ants locate a city on some sunny point near the timbered lands, they do not plant the poppy, but appear to prefer certain trees and vines for shade. For this purpose they plant the seeds of the prairie dogwood (*Viburnum dentatum*), Yopon (*Ilex vomitoria*), Hackberry tree (*Celtis occidentalis*), Gum elastic tree (*Bumelia lycioides*), the mustang grape (*Vitis Texana*), *Cocculus Carolina* and occasionally the prickly ash (*Xanthoxylum fraxinum*)." While there can be little doubt that various herbs, shrubs, or even trees may spring up from the seeds collected and dropped by the ants on the soil of their nests, it is absurd to say that such seeds are actually planted with an awareness that they will ultimately grow and produce shade. Lincecum here repeats the error which he promulgated in regard to the harvesting ants of Texas (*Pogonomyrmex molefaciens*).

Norton (1868) gave a good general description of the Mexican *Atta fervens*, but made no observations on its fungus gardens.

In 1870 B. R. Townsend studied *A. texana* at Austin, Texas. Concerning the leaves collected by this ant he says: "These leaves are conveyed through these underground passages to their homes and deposited in one of their chambers, and, I presume, they secrete some substance that they put with the leaves, for if a handful of the leaves is taken in the hand and squeezed, a ball is made very much resembling coarse bees wax, and when dried is as hard as dry putty. I judge the leaves by their decay produce a gentle heat, or, at least, maintain a uniform temperature whereby the eggs are hatched. Formerly it was suggested that these leaves constituted a store of food, but such is not the case. Whether they feed upon vegetable or animal food I cannot say."

A new epoch in the study of the fungus growing ants was inaugurated by Belt in 1874 in his interesting volume, 'The Naturalist in Nicaragua.' He was the first to surmise the use to which the leaves, etc., are put by the species which he studied (probably *A. cephalotes*). As his work has become rather rare, I quote the pertinent passages in full: "Notwithstanding that these ants are so common throughout tropical America, and have excited the attention of nearly every traveller, there still remains much doubt as to the use to which the leaves are put. Some Naturalists have supposed that they use them directly as food; others, that they roof their underground nests with them. I believe the real use they make of them is as a manure, on which grows a minute species of fungus, on which they feed; — that they are, in reality, mushroom growers and eaters. This explanation is so extraordinary and unexpected, that I may be permitted to enter somewhat at length on the facts that led me to adopt it. When I first began my warfare against the ants that attacked my garden, I dug down deeply into some of their nests. In our mining operations we also, on two occasions, carried our excavations from below up through very large formicariums so that all their underground workings were exposed to observation. I found their nests below to consist of numerous rounded chambers, about as large as a man's head, connected together by tunnelled passages leading from one chamber to another. Notwithstanding that many columns of the ants were continually carrying in the cut leaves, I could never find any quantity of these in the burrows, and it was evident that they were used up in some way immediately they were brought in. The chambers were always about three parts filled with a speckled, brown, flocculent, spongy-looking mass of a light and loosely connected substance. Throughout these masses were numerous ants belonging to the smallest division of the workers, which do not engage in leaf-carrying. Along with them were pupæ and larvæ, not gathered together, but dispersed, apparently irregularly, throughout the flocculent mass. This mass, which I have called the ant-food, proved, on examination to be composed of minutely subdivided pieces of leaves, withered to a brown color, and overgrown and lightly connected together by a minute white fungus that ramified in every direction throughout it. I not only found this fungus in every chamber I opened, but also in the chambers of the nest of a distinct species that generally comes out only in the night-time, often entering houses and carrying off various farinaceous substances, and does not make mounds above its nests, but long winding passages, terminating in chambers similar to the common species and always, like them, three parts filled with flocculent masses of fungus-covered vegetable matter, amongst which are the ant-nurses and immature ants. When a nest is disturbed, and the masses of ant-food spread about, the ants are in great concern to carry away every morsel of it under shelter again; and sometimes, when I dug into a nest, I found the next day all the earth thrown out filled with little pits that the ants had dug into it to get out the covered up food. When they migrate from one part to another, they also carry with them all the ant-food from their old habitations. That they do not eat the leaves themselves I convinced myself, for I found near the tenanted chambers, deserted ones filled with the refuse particles of leaves that had been exhausted as manure for the fungus, and were now left, and served as food for larvæ of *Staphylinidæ* and other beetles.

"These ants do not confine themselves to leaves, but also carry off any vegetable substance that they find suitable for growing fungus on. They are very partial to the inside white rind of oranges, and I have also seen them cutting up and carrying off the flowers of certain shrubs, the leaves of which they have neglected. They are very particular about the ventilation of their underground chambers, and have numerous holes leading up to the surface from them. These they open out or close up, apparently to keep up a regular degree of temperature below. The great care they take that the pieces of leaves they carry into the nest should be neither too dry nor too damp, is also consistent with the idea that the object is the growth of a fungus that requires particular conditions of temperature and moisture to ensure its vigorous growth. If a sudden shower should come on, the ants do not carry the wet pieces into the burrows, but throw them down near the entrances. Should the weather clear up again, these pieces are picked up when nearly dried, and taken inside; should the rain, however, continue, they get sodden down into the ground, and are left there. On the contrary, in dry and hot weather, when the leaves would get dried up before they could be conveyed to the nest, the ants, when in exposed situations, do not go out at all during the hot hours, but bring in their leafy burdens in the cool of the day and during the night. As soon as the pieces of leaves are carried in they must be cut up by the small class of workers into little pieces. I have never seen the smallest class of ants carrying in leaves; their duties appear to be inside, cutting them into smaller fragments, and nursing the immature ants. I have, however, seen them running out along the paths with the others; but instead of helping to carry in the burdens, they climb on the top of the pieces which are being carried along by the middle-sized workers, and so get a ride home again. It is very probable that they take a run out merely for air and exercise. The largest class of what are called workers are, I believe, the directors and protectors of the others. They are never seen out of the nest, excepting on particular occasions, such as the migration of the ants, and when one of the working columns or nests is attacked; they then come stalking up, and attack the enemy with their strong jaws. Sometimes, when digging into the burrows, one of these giants has unperceived climbed up my dress, and the first intimation of his presence has been the burying of his jaws in my neck, from which he would not fail to draw the blood."

During his study of *Atta* in the province of Rio Grande de Sul, Brazil, Fritz Müller appears to have reached independently the same conclusion as Belt. A letter directed to Charles Darwin and published in 'Nature' during 1874 contains the following remarks: "As to the leaf-cutting ants I have always held the same view which is proposed by Mr. Belt, viz. that they feed upon the fungus growing on the leaves they carry into their nests, though I had not yet examined their stomachs. Now I find that the contents of the stomach are colorless showing under the microscope some minute globules, probably the spores of the fungus. I could find no trace of the vegetable tissue which might have been derived from the leaves they gather; and this I think, confirms Mr. Belt's hypothesis."

Although observations on the habits of the Attii continued to be published from time to time the suggestions of Belt and Müller were either overlooked or ignored for nearly twenty years. In his studies on *Atta texana*, which, like those of Buckley, Lincecum and Townsend, were carried on at Austin, Texas, McCook (1879*a*, 1879*b*, etc.) accurately described the formicaries and fungus gardens. He found the nests to consist of several chambers or pockets, sometimes as much as 2 ft. 10 inches long, 12 inches broad and 8 inches high. The fungus gardens within these chambers are correctly described as "masses of a very light, delicate leaf-paper wrought into what may be properly called 'combs.' Some of the masses were in a single hemisphere, filling the central part of the cave, others were arranged in columnar masses 2½ inches high, in contact along the floor. Some of these columns hung, like rude honeycomb or wasp nests from roots which interlaced the chambers. The material was in some cases of a gray tint, in others of a leaf-brown. It was all evidently composed of the fibre of leaves which had been reduced to this form within the nest, probably the joint action of the mandibles and salivary glands. On examination they proved to be composed of cells of various sizes, irregular in shape, but maintaining pretty constantly the hexagon. Some of the cells were one-half inch in diameter, many one-fourth inch, most of them one-eighth inch, and quite minute.

Large circular openings ran into the heart of the mass. Some of the cells were one inch deep; they usually narrowed into a funnel-like cylinder. Ants in great numbers, chiefly of the small castes, were found within these cells. In the first large cave opened were also great numbers of larvæ. The material was so fragile that it crumbled under even delicate handling, but a few specimens of parts of the ant's comb, with entire cells, were preserved and exhibited." Although McCook knew of Belt's opinion that these masses of triturated leaves serve merely as a culture medium for the growth of edible fungi, and even saw the film of hyphæ, he nevertheless preferred to interpret the latter as "only what might have been expected under such environment," and expressed the belief "that the ants feed upon the juices of leaves." He fully appreciated the extraordinary excavating powers of *A. texana.* "The ability of these emmet masons to excavate vast halls and subterranean avenues is remarkable. Several holes in the vicinity of Austin were visited, out of which 'beds' or nests of ants had been dug by an old man who used to follow the business of ant killing. These holes were nearly as large as the cellar for a small house. One such excavation, about three miles from Austin, was 12 feet in diameter and 15 feet deep. At the lowest point had been found the main cavity, quite as large as a flour barrel, in which were found many winged insects, males and females, and quantities of larvæ. This nest was situated 669 feet from a tree that stood in the front yard of a house which the ants had stripped." McCook examined and reconstructed the tunnel excavated by the ants in order to reach this point and found that although its course varied from 18 inches to 6 feet below the surface it deviated little from a direct line and gave off a couple of branch tunnels to a peach orchard 120 feet distant.

In 1880 Morris studied the habits of a small Attiine ant (*Trachymyrmex septentrionalis*) which he had discovered near the village of Tom's River on Barnegat Bay, New Jersey. During December of the same year McCook communicated this discovery to the Philadelphia Academy of Sciences and during the following year (1881) Morris published his own observations in the 'American Naturalist.' Both authors regarded the fungus-gardens as subterranean "combs" adapted for incubating the brood. Morris saw the ants carry in and incorporate into their fungus gardens the leaves of seedling pines, the flowers of cow wheat (*Melampyrum americanum*) and "the droppings of certain larvæ that feed on oak-leaves." The nest is described by both authors and figured by McCook as consisting of two spherical chambers, one above the other and connected by a short gallery. The entrance was oblique and about 2 inches in length. The upper chamber was 1½ inches in diameter, the lower 3 inches. The former was empty, the latter contained the "combs" suspended from rootlets that had been left intact while the ants were excavating the chamber.   Morris's description of these "combs" is more accurate than McCook's.

Brent in 1886 described the nesting habits, etc., of the large *Atta cephalotes* of Trinidad: "A good sized mango tree, at least as large as an average apple tree, I saw stripped of every leaf in one night, and greater feats than this are recorded of these 'Fourmi Ciseaux,' as they are called by the Creoles." Brent gives a diagram of the nest and describes a tunnel leading from the lowermost fungus-chamber to a still lower level.   He "invariably found this lower tunnel wherever the inclination permitted its construction" and has "no doubt that it is constructed as a drain, and that the ants know as much about the advantage of thorough drainage as they have been proved to know, by many eminent observers, of those of other sanitary matters." Some of the chambers of the nest are described as 3 feet in diameter.   He mentions Amphisbænians as living in the nest and eating the ants.   In regard to the use to which the leaves are put, Brent says: "A solution of arseniate of soda was next sprinkled upon orange leaves, which were strewn upon the mound.   These were eventually cleared away, although at an immense sacrifice of life.   This points, I think, to the true ant food, since unless the juices of the leaves as they were sawed up were swallowed, the poison would have no effect.   This idea is strengthened by the fact that fiery and strongly aromatic plants as well as those with poisonous, milky juices are carefully avoided.   No solid food is found in the crops of the insect at any time, but if these are examined after the insects have been engaged in leaf-cutting, they are found full of green leaf juice."   Later he says: "The larvæ are embedded in a soft woolly matter which proved to be the finely masticated parenchyma of the leaves.   Thus a use was found for the leaves, although it reflects seriously upon the supposed sagacity of the ants that they should procure so many more than are required for the purpose."

Emery (1890) appended a brief ethological note to his description of *Acromyrmex landolti* of Caracas, Venezuela.   Simon wrote him that "this ant makes extensive formicaries with several entrances, each surmounted by a column or chimney of straws 10–15 cm. high, in which lives a large spider of the genus *Ctenus*.   Simon never saw the ants carry in pieces of leaves like *Atta sexdens* and believes that they confine themselves to collecting pieces of dried grasses."

Observations on *A. cephalotes* in Trinidad were resumed in 1892 by Tanner in two important papers, which, owing to their publication in an obscure serial, have been overlooked by subsequent students.   He was the first to study Attii in artificial nests and to prove that not only the adult ants but also the larvæ feed on fungus hyphæ.   In his first paper (1892a) he describes the manner in which the workers triturate the leaves: "Each forager drops the portion of the leaf in the nest, which is taken up as required by the small workers, and carried to a clear space in the nest to be cleaned. This is done with their mandibles, and if considered too large it is cut into smaller pieces. It is then taken in hand by the large workers, who lick it with their tongues. Then comes the most important part, which almost always is done by the larger workers, who manipulate it between their mandibles, mostly standing on three legs. The portion of the leaf is turned round and round between the mandibles, the ant using her palpi, tongue, her three legs and her antennæ while doing so. It now becomes a small almost black ball, varying in size from a mustard seed to the finest dust shot, according to the size of the piece of the leaf that has been manipulated. The size of the piece of the leaf is from $\frac{1}{8}$ by $\frac{1}{8}$ of an inch, to $\frac{1}{4}$ by $\frac{1}{4}$ of an inch. I do not wish it to be understood that only one class of workers manipulate the leaf, for all seem to take to it very kindly on emergency. Even the smallest workers will bring their tiny ball to where the fungus bed is being prepared. These balls, really pulp, are built on to an edge of the fungus bed by the larger workers, and are slightly smoothed down as the work proceeds. The new surface is then planted by the smaller workers, by slips of the fungus brought from the older parts of the nest. Each plant is planted separately and they know exactly how far apart the plants should be. It sometimes looks as if the plants had been put in too scantily in places, yet in about 40 hours if the humidity has been properly regulated, it is all evenly covered with a mantle as of very fine snow. It is the fungus they eat, and with small portions of it the workers feed the larvæ."

In his second paper, published the same year (December, 1892), Tanner describes the eggs and larvæ of *A. cephalotes* and the method of feeding the latter, together with certain observations which go to show that workers lay eggs capable of developing into other workers or even queens. The eggs become enveloped in a "pearly white fluffy growth." The larvæ which hatch from these eggs "are usually placed on the top of the nest and are constantly attended by the smallest workers — the nurses — who separate them into divisions according to their size. At first it seemed a mystery, how these minute grubs could be fed so systematically, knowing that each individual larva was only one among so many, yet certain it was, that all were equally attended to. Further observations showed that nature had provided most efficiently for them to ask for food when they required it. This the larvæ do by pouting their lips; at this notification of their requirement the first nurse who happens to be passing stops and feeds them. The nurses are continually moving about among them with pieces of fungus in their mouths ready for a call for food. The nurses feed the minute larvæ by merely brushing the fungus across their lips showing that the spores alone are sufficient for its food at that period of its life. But it is not so when the larvæ have increased so much in size, that the pout can be seen without a glass, for then the whole piece after having been manipulated by the nurse's mandibles into a ball, in the same manner as the leaves are served, when they are first brought into the nest, is placed in its throat and if that is not sufficient the pout continues when the next one and even the next passing proceeds with the feeding, till the pout is withdrawn, showing that it is satisfied. No further notice is then taken of it by the feeders, until it agains asks for a meal by pouting later on in the day."

In 1893 a nephew of the celebrated Fritz Müller, Alfred Mœller, who was given a grant of 5,000 marks by the Berlin Academy of Sciences for the purpose of studying the habits of the Attii at Blumenau in the province of Rio Grande do Sul, published the most important of existing works on these insects and their relations to the fungi which they cultivate. He studied several species of *Atta* belonging to the subgenus *Acromyrmex* (*discigera, coronata, octospinosa, mœlleri*) and of the genera *Apterostigma* (*pilosum, mœlleri, wasmanni*, and an undetermined species) and *Cyphomyrmex* (*auritus, strigatus*). *A. octospinosa* and *discigera*, which nest in the woods, form truncated cones of dead leaves and twigs, beneath which they excavate a single chamber containing a large fungus garden sometimes $1\frac{1}{2}$ meters long. *A. mœlleri* has similar habits, but *coronata* resembles the species of the subgenus *Atta* s. str. in forming several chambers, each with its own fungus garden. In all of these species the garden is built up on the floor of the chamber in the form of a loose sponge-work of triturated leaf-fragments permeated with fungus hyphæ which he describes as follows: "Over all portions of the surface of the garden are seen round, white corpuscles about $\frac{1}{4}$ mm. in diameter on an average, although some of them are fully $\frac{1}{2}$ mm. and sometimes adjacent corpuscles fuse to form masses 1 mm. across and of irregular form. After a little experience one learns to detect these corpuscles with the naked eye as pale, white points which are everywhere abundant in all the nests. Under the lens they sometimes have a glistening appearance like drops of water. They are absent from the youngest, most recently established portions of the garden, but elsewhere uniformly distributed, so that it is impossible to remove with the fingers a particle too small to contain some of the white bodies. I call these the 'kohlrabi clusters' of the ants' nests. They constitute the principal, if not the only food of the species of *Atta*." These clusters are made up of the "heads of Kohlrabi," which are small terminal dilatations of the hyphæ of a spherical or oval form. Mœller confirmed Belt's observations on the solicitude of the ants for their gardens, and showed that these insects in artificial nests will completely rebuild these structures within 12 hours after they have been disintegrated or scattered. He also saw the ants eating the fungus and was able to satisfy himself that the different species of *Atta* will eat the Kohlrabi from one another's colonies but not that of *Apterostigma* or *Cyphomyrmex*. He gives the following interesting description of the way in which the leaves are comminuted by the workers. "The manipulation of the pieces of leaves is the same in all the *Atta* species and the following description holds good uniformly for all of them. The ant first cuts the leaf it has brought in through the middle and then busies itself with only one of the halves, cutting off another piece, and so on. When the piece of leaf which it has retained is sufficiently small so that it can be turned round and round between its fore-feet with the aid of its jaws, it is felt of on all sides and turned in all directions as if the insect wished to get a clear idea of its form. Then an even smaller piece is cut off and this is repeated, till the piece that is retained is hardly longer than the ant's head. The rejected pieces are picked up by other workers and treated in the same manner. Then the ant holds the little piece between its fore-feet with the sharp edge directed towards its mouth and begins to pinch its edges at short intervals around the circumference without ever cutting through the substance. The piece thus manipulated shows fine, radial ridges under a good lens. The surface of the leaf is also abraded with the points of the mandibles, wounded, so to speak, so that it soon becomes soft. Then the ant kneads it with the feet and again inserts her jaws into the pellet thus formed in order to mould it thoroughly. Again and again the jaws close upon the pellet while the feet press it and place it in a new position, and again it is kneaded. This manipulation is carried on with great care and deliberation, and I have several times observed that an ant will spend a quarter of an hour in making such a pellet. When it has become a soft mass, the worker takes it in her jaws and seeks a suitable spot for it in the portion of the garden that is just being built. Once I saw an ant that had found such a spot, actually jab the pellet into the garden with a jerk of her head and a simultaneous opening of her jaws, and then carefully pat it down with her fore-feet. Another time a worker laid her pellet in a breach of a newly erected circular wall, and then shook and pushed it into the depression, like a mason setting the last brick in a fresh layer of mortar. During all of this work, the antennæ are continually moving and palpating the pellet just as they are while the ant is feeding." Into the new material thus added to the garden the fungus hyphæ grow very rapidly. By afternoon pellets built in during the morning hours have become permeated in all directions with mycelium. Belt supposed that the smallest workers or minims comminute the leaves and build up the fungus gardens. According to Mœller, however, this is the office of the mediæ, as the leaves are too thick to be manipulated by the smallest workers. The latter have another function, namely that of weeding the garden and keeping down the growth of spores belonging to alien fungi. Mœller emphasizes the remarkable fact that the gardens are pure cultures although the hairy, rough-bodied workers must be continually bringing into the nest all sorts of spores and bacteria. It is probable also, that the minims are instrumental in producing the "kohlrabi heads" as these are not developed when the mycelium is grown in artificial culture media apart from the influence of the ants. He summarizes the results of this portion of his studies in the following words: "All the fungus-gardens of the *Atta* species I have investigated, are pervaded with the same kind of mycelium, which produces the 'kohlrabi clusters' as long as the ants are cultivating the gardens. Under the influence of the ants neither free aërial hyphæ nor any form of fruit are ever developed. The mycelium proliferates through the garden to the complete exclusion of any alien fungus, and the fungus garden of a nest represents in its entirety a pure culture of a single fungus. The fungus has two different forms of conidia which arise in the garden when it is removed from the influence of the ants. The hyphæ have a very pronounced tendency to produce swellings or diverticula, which show several more or less peculiar and clearly differentiated variations. One of these which has presumably reached its present form through the influence of cultivation and selection on the part of the ants, is represented by the 'kohlrabi heads'."

A number of experiments were undertaken by Mœller for the purpose of ascertaining the behavior of the fungus in the absence of the ants. Under these conditions he found that the mycelium produces aërial hyphæ, the "kohlrabi clusters" and "heads" disappear and soon the fungus breaks up into masses of bead-like conidia. "As long as the ants are active in their garden, there is never either in it or in its immediate vicinity the slightest trace of an alien fungus, and, under these circumstances, the mycelium pervading the garden never produces aërial hyphæ or conidia." If, however, a few of the ants happen to be left in the garden, the development of aërial hyphæ is retarded, and though Mœller did not observe the process directly, he is certain that these hyphæ must be bitten off by the ants as soon as they make their appearance. "A relatively very small number of workers suffices to restrain the growth of the aërial hyphæ. But if the number is too small, the aërial filaments begin to appear sporadically. The ants are unable to move about in the dense growth of sprouting filaments and have to beat a retreat before the rapidly rising hyphal forest. This, however, as soon as it has acquired a little headway, proliferates mightily, and it is an amazing sight to behold the poor insects, tirelessly active till the last moment, fleeing before their own food-plant. If some of the larvæ and pupæ are still present, they are rescued.   The last resort is the vertical wall of the glass, up which the insects creep and where they huddle together, while over the wide plain of the garden the fungus proceeds to the conidia-producing stage."

Mœller next undertook to determine the systematic position of the fungus. He naturally supposed that the discovery of the fruiting form would show it to be an asco- or basidiomycete.   Although he failed to raise either of these forms from his mycelial cultures he succeeded on four occasions in finding an undescribed agaricine mushroom with wine-red stem and pileus growing on extinct or abandoned *Acromyrmex* nests.   From the basidiospores of this plant which he called *Rozites gongylophora,* he succeeded in raising a mycelium resembling in all respects that of the ant gardens.   Three of the species of *Acromyrmex* did not hesitate to eat portions both of this mycelium and of the pileus and stem of the *Rozites.*   He believed therefore that he had definitely established the specific identity of the fungus cultivated by the ants.

The species of *Apterostigma* investigated by Mœller usually nest in cavities in rotten wood which is often also inhabited by other insects.   The fine wood castings and excrement of these insects are used by the ants as material with which to construct their fungus-gardens.   *A. wasmanni* constructs the largest nests, and it is only in the gardens of this species that the mycelium produces structures analogous to the "kohlrabi heads" and "clusters" of *Acromyrmex.*   The heads, however, are club-shaped instead of spherical dilatations of the hyphæ.   As it produces only irregular swellings on the hyphæ Mœller believes that *Apterostigma* represents a much lower stage in fungus-culture than the species of *Acromyrmex.*   The *Apterostigma* are, however, very adaptable since they readily collect caterpillar excrement or even farina and incorporate these substances into their gardens.   Mœller states that all the species of this genus cultivate the same fungus, which must be a distinct species as the ants will not eat the fungus grown by *Acromyrmex.*   The gardens of *pilosum, mœlleri* and another undetermined *Apterostigma,* which live in small colonies of only 12 to 20 individuals, are suspended from the roofs of the small cavities, 3 to 4 cm. in diameter, in the rotten wood and exhibit a peculiar structure not seen in other *Attii.* "The garden is often completely, or at least nearly always in great part, enclosed in a white cob-web-like membrane.   It was often possible to obtain a view of uninjured nests of *A. pilosum* that had been excavated in clefts of the rotten wood.   In such cases the envelope enclosed the whole fungus garden like a bag with only a single orifice or entrance.   The envelope is attached in a pendent position to the surrounding wood, roots or particles of earth by means of radiating fibres, and this explains why the gardens

...ays excavated in clayey soil, and the raised entrances, which
...ss cylindrical, are constructed with the particles of earth result-
...mining operations and are about an inch in height. In young
...entrance leads into a small chamber, about six inches below
... the ground, situated not at the end of the gallery but either
...ight of it. As the colony increases the ants do not enlarge this
...ber, but, piercing its side, form another chamber near it with
...nce hole. In large colonies, which never consist of more than
...dividuals, a nest consists of two or three chambers which open
...al excavation. This is no longer used for growing the fungus
...s a sort of ante-chamber which generally contains material
... the ants to grow their mushrooms on, which is deposited here
... made use of. The chambers adjoining are more or less round,
...ter of about 2–3 inches, and any small roots of plants growing
... are not cut away but used by the ants to hang their mushroom
... These fill the interior of the chamber and consist of a gray
... consisting of a great number of little irregular cells and resem-
...se sponge, amongst which are scattered larvæ, pupæ and ants.
... the cells consist of small round pellets resembling dust shot and
...ed by and enveloped in white fungus hyphæ, which hold the
...er. Strewn thickly upon the surface of the garden are to be
...white bodies about a quarter of a millimeter in diameter. These
...œller terms "Kohlrabi" clumps, and consist of an aggregation
...ith special swellings at their ends. It is on this that the ants
...fungus found by Mœller in the nests of the Brazilian fungus
...romyrmex) is the *Rozites gongylophora*, Mœller, and if it is not
...ecies cultivated by *S. opacus* it is, at any rate, very nearly related
...aterial to grow their mushrooms on the ants make use of particles
...wers, and leaves, but prefer fruit. They do well in artificial
...ructed on Sir John Lubbock's plan, and are easy to watch. I
...hem with all kinds of vegetable products; they have taken orange,
...se petals and leaves and once they even made use of the dried
...he back of an old book lying near their nest, but that day they
...g else; if the choice be left to them they invariably take fruit and
...fer the orange amongst these. Very small particles of the white
... oranges are torn off, and after undergoing a slight kneading
...the ants' mandibles, are planted in the nest. The neuters are
...ame size, varying but slightly and never exceed 4 mm. in length.
...nore diurnal in their habits than other species of fungus growers,—
...ork a little at night. I have found winged forms in the nests in
...of July."

are so easily torn asunder while the nest is being uncovered." Even in
captivity these ants persisted in hanging their gardens to the sides of the
glass dishes in which they were kept. "Microscopical examination shows
that the envelope consists of the same, loop-like hyphæ as the remainder
of the garden. Such a structure cannot be produced by the fungus except
under extraneous influences. We must assume that the ants bring about
the development of the envelope, that they direct or coërce the growth of
individual hyphæ with their antennæ or fore legs, spread them out into a
layer and bite off the recalcitrant hyphæ that grow out from the surface."
Mœller succeeded in cultivating the mycelium of the *Apterostigma* gardens
in artificial media, but he failed to obtain the fruiting stage. He believes,
however, that the fungus is a basidiomycete.

The two species of *Cyphomyrmex* observed by Mœller were found nesting
under bark or in rotten wood like *Apterostigma*. The largest gardens
of *C. strigatus* are only 8 cm. long, whereas those of *C. auritus* may attain
a length of 15 cm. and a breadth and height of 5 cm. These gardens are
never pendent and never enclosed in a mycelial envelope. In other respects
they resemble those of *Apterostigma* and are grown on the same substrata.
The heads are developed as long, irregular swellings in the hyphæ and
therefore represent a more primitive and imperfect stage than those of
Acromyrmex. Although he was unable to obtain the fruiting stage, Mœller
nevertheless believed that the fungus of the species of *Cyphomyrmex* is
different from that cultivated by the ants of other genera. He concludes
his paper with a few interesting notes on the breeding habits of the Attii.
The eggs of *Acromyrmex* are laid in masses and embedded in loosely woven
hyphæ which enable the ants to carry them about in packets. The pupæ,
too, are often enclosed in hyphæ, but this is not the case with the larvæ which
are kept clean and shining.

In 1894 von Ihering, in an interesting paper on the ants of Rio Grande do
Sul, records a number of observations on Attii (*Atta sexdens*, *Mœllerius
striatus*, *Acromyrmex lundi*, *niger* and *Cyphomyrmex morschi*). His general
account of the nests of *A. sexdens* agrees with that of preceding authors
who have studied the large *Attæ* s. str., and comprises also an interesting
observation quoted from a former paper (1882) on the importance of these
insects in reversing the position of earth strata: "A piece of pasture land
had been marked off by a recently excavated ditch several feet deep. The
soil in this place, as generally in the surrounding country, consisted of sand.
Beneath this in many portions of the region there was a stratum of heavy
red clay at a depth of four feet or more. What attracted my attention in
this ditch was the fact that here the clay lay uppermost in a layer about 1 dcm.
thick. The explanation of this condition was not the result of geological

but of zoölogical investigation, for closer inspection soon showed that the ants are responsible for the inversion of the normal position of the strata. It was the work of *Atta sexdens*. It is very doubtful whether such an enormous task can be accomplished by any insects except the large species of *Atta*." Von Ihering observed the marriage flight of *A. sexdens* and the digging of the nests by the recently fertilized females, an instinct manifested even by individuals whose gasters have been bitten off by birds. *A. sexdens* extends southward in Brazil only to the Cebus-line (latitude 30°) The nests of *Acromyrmex lundi* are excavated to a depth of 50–60 cm. and consist of a single chamber with a cubic capacity of $\frac{1}{2}$ to 1 litre, in older nests 5 to 10 times as great. This cavity contains a single fungus garden and is connected with the surface by means of a large horizontal or tortuous gallery 1–2 m. long. From the nest-entrance, branching, well-worn roads lead off over the surface often to a distance of 40 m. and further, and it is along these that the ants travel to and from the grasses which they cut down together with their green seeds. This ant carries the exhausted portions of the fungus garden out of the nest and deposits them on a refuse heap. The same is true of *Mollerius striatus*. This species clears the ground of vegetation around its nest entrance which is surmounted by a crater. Like *A. lundi* it collects pieces of grass, flowers, leaves, etc. *A. niger* nests in thickets between the roots, where it excavates its nest at some distance from the entrance. It does not confine its cutting operations largely to grasses like *lundi* and *striatus* but attacks many other plants and is therefore of greater economic importance.

Cyphomyrmex morschi nests in the soil, where it excavates a chamber about the size of an orange and containing a fungus garden of leaf detritus covered with mycelium. The entrance is surmounted by a circular crater.

Von Ihering is one of the few who have considered the question of the origin of the fungus-raising instincts of the Attii. His remarks on this subject will be considered in the concluding portion of this article.

Urich, in two papers published during the same year (1895a, 1895b) records a number of observations on several of the Attii of Trinidad (*Atta sexdens, A. cephalotes, Acromyrmex octospinosus, Trachymyrmex urichi, Sericomyrmex opacus, Apterostigma urichi, A. mayri* and *Cyphomyrmex rimosus*). His account of the large species of *Atta* adds little of interest to that of previous authors. On two occasions he found the deälated females of *Acromyrmex octospinosus* "working just as hard and engaged in the same occupation as the neuters, viz: cutting leaves and carrying them to the nest. They all issued from the same nest and therefore could not have been mothers of new colonies." He "also noticed that several females lost their wings in the nest without any marital flight, although a few weeks later the winged ones swarmed out in the usual way on a damp evening."

The nest of *Trachymyrmex uri* never anywhere else. It consists o a foot and is never directly under side at right angles and about 9 inches ing the particles of earth which res way from the entrance hole, say abou conical heap.... These ants also cult *gongylophora* it is very much like it. the ants' chamber are not cut away, bu gardens which are in their case regula turnal in habits and when disturbed small fallen flowers and the fruit of v gardens, but at the same time they d the young and tender shoots. They a slow in their movements."

The habits of *Apterostigma urichi* *Atta* this species does not excavate its ne of trees.... They are built in hanging p from the top, but never let the nest touc the garden is quite recent and small it is covering, which at first sight looks like fi bottom. The nests therefore look like a never larger than an apple. On break small mushroom garden is found consist ants, larvæ and pupæ are scattered." Th by Mœller for the Brazilian species of always found under rotten wood and the a of wood-boring insects as a medium for g colonies of these ants are small, not num brown workers, all of about the same size, vi long legs which measure 7–7$\frac{1}{2}$ mm. without habits." The smaller *A. mayri* constructs not only under rotten wood but also unde the excrement of wood-boring insects, but is of flowers. The mycelium has the kohlrabi and according to Urich represents a more a *A. urichi*. The ants are nocturnal and sham

Urich has also given us the only existii *Sericomyrmex* (*S. opacus*). "The nests of t about Port of Spain, in gardens, in the grass flower beds, and from their peculiar raised ent

They are alw are more or le ing from their colonies this the surface o to the left or original chan a small entra about 200 in on the origin in, but form brought in b and graduall with a diam through ther gardens on. spongy mass bling a coar The walls of are penetrat mass togeth seen round are what M of hyphæ w feed. The growers (A the same sp to it. As of fruit, fl nests, cons have tried t banana, ro glue from had nothin seem to pr skin of th process in all of the s They are but also w the month

Urich is responsible for the erroneous statement that *Cyphomyrmex rimosus* "does not cultivate any fungus," a statement which has been repeated by subsequent writers (Forel, Emery).

In 1896 Swingle read a paper on *Trachymyrmex septentrionalis* (= *tardigrada* auct.) before the American Association for the Advancement of Science. He says: "In July of this year I examined some colonies of *Atta tardigrada*, which Mr. Pergande had found in the vicinity of Washington. The nests are small subterranean cavities, 6–10 cm. in diameter, situated from 2 to 15 or 20 cm. below the surface. Some nests have one cavity, others two. Almost the whole cavity is filled with a grayish material loosely and irregularly connected together. By watching the ants, it was determined that they carried into their nests the excrements of some leaf-eating insect, lying on the ground under neighboring oak-trees. The same material was found to constitute at least a large part of the substance filling the nest. Even with a low magnifying lens, tufts of minute sparkling bodies could be seen on the fragments of the fungus garden, while the whole mass was interpenetrated by the white mycelium of a fungus. Examination with higher magnification showed that the glistening tufts were really composed of 'Kohlrabi' even more perfectly spherical than figured by M. Mœller. The mature 'Kohlrabi' were very much larger than the mycelium below, being 22 to 52 μ wide and 30 to 56 μ long, while the supporting mycelial threads were only 4 to 8 μ in diameter. There are no septa dividing the 'Kohlrabis' from the mycelial threads. The whole appearance of the fungus is strikingly similar to that found by Mœller, and it is by no means impossible that it will prove to be the same species though the Kohlrabis are nearly twice as large as what he reports."

Forel (1896*a–c*, 1897, 1899–1900*b*) has recorded a number of observations on the *Attii* of Colombia (*A. sexdens, cephalotes* and *lævigata*; *Acromyrmex octospinosus*, and species of *Trachymyrmex, Sericomyrmex, Mycocepurus*, and *Apterostigma*). He excavated one of the huge nests of *A. sexdens* belonging to an extensive colony at Rio Frio (1896*b*). "This nest looked like an immature volcano and consisted of a mass of 12 to 20 fused craters. The whole nest was 5 or 6 m. in diameter and about 1 m. high. The largest (median) crater was about 60 cm. in diameter, 28 cm. high, and had an opening below of about $3\frac{1}{2}$ cm. The smaller accessory nests in the neighborhood (100 to 200 steps distant) had only 2–3 craters and were much smaller. There are two kinds of craters; one consisting of sand or soil of a gray color and consisting of the excavated earth, the others are brown and consist of the rejected and useless remains of the gardens, *i. e.*, the portions that have been exhausted by the fungi, thrown out in this manner in the form of brown pellets. The medium-sized workers are

seen continually coming out of the latter craters laden with brown pellets
which they cast aside, while into the gray craters a stream of the same kind
of workers is entering in an almost continuous procession laden with green
leaves. Some small workers also stand around the openings. On disturbing the nest one is severely attacked by the largest workers. With their
sharp jaws, worked by enormous muscles, they can bite so severely as to
bring the blood; in fact, a small artery in my little finger was severed by
one of these workers. The wounds were as much as 4 mm. in length.
Nevertheless Mr. Bradbury, a native and myself attacked the nest with a
shovel and dug into it deeply. Thousands of the large workers rushed out
at us. The half-naked Indian ran away and I had to retreat from time
to time with bleeding hands. But the interior of the nest was laid bare.
This consisted of a number of great cavities, 15 to 20 cm. long and 8–12 cm.
high and each was nearly always filled with a fungus garden, which looks
very much like the single garden of the *Acromyrmex* species. In the labyrinth of this gray to brown garden live thousands of the smallest and medium
sized workers, together with the whole ant brood. Colossal female larvæ
are there found covered with a regular envelope of larvæ of all sizes, so that
they have the appearance of hedge hogs. The workers held fast to the
larvæ so tenaciously that I could take them in my hands and even kill them
in alcohol without their losing their hold....The large species of *Atta*
therefore have not only one but hundreds of fungus gardens. The fungus
chambers communicate with one another by means of broad galleries 2–3
cm. in diameter. The lower portion of the garden is uniformly light rust-
red with white fungus patches, whereas the upper portions are more gray.
The dark brown portions seem to represent the residuum. The fungus
garden is so friable that it is impossible to remove it without destroying its
form. How the old myth, or nonsense, that these *Atta* species line their
nests with leaves could have originated and could even be revamped by
McCook is incomprehensible to me....All the pupæ are naked, that is,
not enclosed in cocoons. The workers have the habit of carrying their
straying sisters exactly like our species of *Formica* (the carried ant is rolled
under the head of the carrier)." In another place (1899, 1900*b*) Forel says
that *Acromyrmex octospinosus* carries its sister workers in the reverse position, *i. e.*, like *Myrmica*. He also describes (1896*b*) very briefly the nests
and distribution of *A. cephalotes* and *lævigata*. The latter also has very
large but deeply subterranean nests. It lives more in the mountains at and
above an altitude of 1,000 m. and so far down in the ground that Forel could
not reach the fungus gardens. *Cephalotes* is intermediate; its nests are
nearly as large as those of *sexdens* and the fungus-gardens have a very
similar structure and arrangement. The colonies of *cephalotes* and espe-

cially of *lœvigata,* are less populous than those of *sexdens.* The nests of *cephalotes* occur from sea-level to an altitude of more than 1,000 m., those of *sexdens* only in the low-lying regions.

According to von Ihering (1898) the nest of the Brazilian *Atta sexdens* differs from that of the Colombian form described by Forel. It consists of from one to two dozen chambers, each 25–30 cm. in diameter and 12 to 15 cm. high, with a flat floor and arched ceiling. Each of these chambers, *panellas* (pots) or *pratos* (plates) as they are called by the Brazilians, has one or more, rarely two, galleries entering it at the side and connecting it with the other cavities and the vertical shafts leading to the surface of the nest. The chambers are ½ to 1 m. apart and are excavated at a depth of 4 to 6 m. below the surface or even lower. The fungus gardens are built up on the flat floors of the chambers. Von Ihering found that when the nests are inundated the ants at once remove portions of their fungus gardens to higher ground. When this is impracticable or the inundation is very great, the population of the nest forms a ball held together by the closed jaws of the workers and enclosing in its interior a portion of the fungus garden and probably also the queen. This ball then floats on the water till carried ashore, when the ants land and start a new nest out of reach of the flood. Von Ihering says that his neighbor took advantage of this habit, which by the way is also exhibited by several other tropical ants (*Anomma, Solenopsis geminata,* etc.), to free his premises from the leaf-cutting *Attœ,* by rowing about in his canoe, catching up the floating balls and throwing them into a bucket of boiling water. Von Ihering also gives an interesting account of the *iças,* or virgin queens of *Atta sexdens.* At the time of swarming these are captured in great numbers by the Brazilians. The iça hunter stations himself at the entrance of the nest with his feet in a tub of water in order to protect himself from the savage soldiers and workers, and collects the females while they are issuing from the galleries. A successful catch may yield as many as 12 to 20 litres. The gasters of these iças, removed from the thoraces, legs and heads and roasted with salt, garlic and mandioca meal are eaten as a delicacy ("*passoca*") in many parts of Brazil.

Forel (1899–1900*a,* 1901) has also recorded a few notes on the fungus-gardens of a colony of *Trachymyrmex septentrionalis* which he observed at Black Mountain, North Carolina, but he adds little to the above cited descriptions of Morris, McCook and Swingle. Forel (1905) later published some notes of Gœldi on the nests of *Acromyrmex octospinosus,* the fungus gardens of which are built over the stems of plants and fully exposed to the air in the damp forests of Para. Two photographs accompanying the article show that this fungus garden consists of a number of separate portions unlike the single garden which Urich and Forel describe this ant as making when nesting in the ground.

In 1900 Moreno published some observations on the Mexican *Atta* (probably *fervens*) but these add nothing of value to what was previously known.

In 1901 I recorded a few notes on *Atta fervens* and *Cyphomyrmex rimosus dentatus* which I observed in Mexico. I was able to convince myself that the statements of Urich, Forel and Emery to the effect that the latter species makes no fungus-garden, are erroneous. This ant constructs a fungus garden with caterpillar excrement and cultivates a peculiar fungus consisting of small yellow nodules, which have been overlooked by previous investigators. More recently (1905*a*) I have found that other varieties and subspecies of *C. rimosus* in Texas, Florida, the Bahamas, Porto Rico and Culebra have the same habit. In this same paper I also described briefly the habits of *Trachymyrmex jamaicensis*, and in a subsequent paper (1905*b*) also those of *T. septentrionalis*. A fuller account of these various species will be found in the third part of the present article.

M. T. Cook (1906) has very recently studied the habits of *Atta insularis* and has published a few notes on the ravages of this ant in the plantations of Cuba.

The preceding paragraphs deal almost exclusively with observations on adult colonies of the *Attii* and the constitution and care of their fungus gardens. As soon as these habits had been demonstrated, the question naturally arose as to how the ants first come into possession of the fungi which they cultivate with such marvellous skill and assiduity. The labors of the South American naturalists Sampaio, von Ihering, Gœldi and Jakob Huber have supplied the answer to this interesting question.

Sampaio (1894) on digging up an *Atta* female ten days after the nuptial flight, found her in a cavity with two small white masses, one consisting of 50–60 eggs, the other of a filamentous substance which was the young fungus garden, though not recognized as such. Three and one half months after the nuptial flight he excavated another nest which had an opening to the surface of the soil. He found numerous workers of three different sizes but all smaller than the corresponding castes in adult colonies. They were already cutting leaves and had a fungus garden about 30 cubic centimeters in volume. He estimated the number of workers at 150 to 170, that of the larvæ and pupæ at about 150 and the eggs at 50.

The much more important observations of von Ihering (1898), including his brilliant discovery of the method of transfer of the fungus culture from the maternal to the daughter colony, deserve fuller consideration. According to this observer there are repeated nuptial flights of the Brazilian *Atta sexdens* from the end of October to the middle of December. These flights are essentially like those of other ants. On descending to the earth the are so easily torn asunder while the nest is being uncovered." Even in captivity these ants persisted in hanging their gardens to the sides of the glass dishes in which they were kept. "Microscopical examination shows that the envelope consists of the same, loop-like hyphæ as the remainder of the garden. Such a structure cannot be produced by the fungus except under extraneous influences. We must assume that the ants bring about the development of the envelope, that they direct or coërce the growth of individual hyphæ with their antennæ or fore legs, spread them out into a layer and bite off the recalcitrant hyphæ that grow out from the surface." Mœller succeeded in cultivating the mycelium of the *Apterostigma* gardens in artificial media, but he failed to obtain the fruiting stage. He believes, however, that the fungus is a basidiomycete.

The two species of *Cyphomyrmex* observed by Mœller were found nesting under bark or in rotten wood like *Apterostigma*. The largest gardens of *C. strigatus* are only 8 cm. long, whereas those of *C. auritus* may attain a length of 15 cm. and a breadth and height of 5 cm. These gardens are never pendent and never enclosed in a mycelial envelope. In other respects they resemble those of *Apterostigma* and are grown on the same substrata. The heads are developed as long, irregular swellings in the hyphæ and therefore represent a more primitive and imperfect stage than those of *Acromyrmex*. Although he was unable to obtain the fruiting stage, Mœller nevertheless believed that the fungus of the species of *Cyphomyrmex* is different from that cultivated by the ants of other genera. He concludes his paper with a few interesting notes on the breeding habits of the Attii. The eggs of *Acromyrmex* are laid in masses and embedded in loosely woven hyphæ which enable the ants to carry them about in packets. The pupæ, too, are often enclosed in hyphæ, but this is not the case with the larvæ which are kept clean and shining.

In 1894 von Ihering, in an interesting paper on the ants of Rio Grande do Sul, records a number of observations on Attii (*Atta sexdens, Mœllerius striatus, Acromyrmex lundi, niger* and *Cyphomyrmex morschi*). His general account of the nests of *A. sexdens* agrees with that of preceding authors who have studied the large *Attæ* s. str., and comprises also an interesting observation quoted from a former paper (1882) on the importance of these insects in reversing the position of earth strata: "A piece of pasture land had been marked off by a recently excavated ditch several feet deep. The soil in this place, as generally in the surrounding country, consisted of sand. Beneath this in many portions of the region there was a stratum of heavy red clay at a depth of four feet or more. What attracted my attention in this ditch was the fact that here the clay lay uppermost in a layer about 1 dcm. thick. The explanation of this condition was not the result of geological but of zoölogical investigation, for closer inspection soon showed that the ants are responsible for the inversion of the normal position of the strata. It was the work of *Atta sexdens*. It is very doubtful whether such an enormous task can be accomplished by any insects except the large species of *Atta*." Von Ihering observed the marriage flight of *A. sexdens* and the digging of the nests by the recently fertilized females, an instinct manifested even by individuals whose gasters have been bitten off by birds. *A. sexdens* extends southward in Brazil only to the Cebus-line (latitude 30°) The nests of *Acromyrmex lundi* are excavated to a depth of 50–60 cm. and consist of a single chamber with a cubic capacity of ½ to 1 litre, in older nests 5 to 10 times as great. This cavity contains a single fungus garden and is connected with the surface by means of a large horizontal or tortuous gallery 1–2 m. long. From the nest-entrance, branching, well-worn roads lead off over the surface often to a distance of 40 m. and further, and it is along these that the ants travel to and from the grasses which they cut down together with their green seeds. This ant carries the exhausted portions of the fungus garden out of the nest and deposits them on a refuse heap. The same is true of *Mollerius striatus*. This species clears the ground of vegetation around its nest entrance which is surmounted by a crater. Like *A. lundi* it collects pieces of grass, flowers, leaves, etc. *A. niger* nests in thickets between the roots, where it excavates its nest at some distance from the entrance. It does not confine its cutting operations largely to grasses like *lundi* and *striatus* but attacks many other plants and is therefore of greater economic importance.

Cyphomyrmex morschi nests in the soil, where it excavates a chamber about the size of an orange and containing a fungus garden of leaf detritus covered with mycelium. The entrance is surmounted by a circular crater.

Von Ihering is one of the few who have considered the question of the origin of the fungus-raising instincts of the Attii. His remarks on this subject will be considered in the concluding portion of this article.

Urich, in two papers published during the same year (1895*a*, 1895*b*) records a number of observations on several of the Attii of Trinidad (*Atta sexdens*, *A. cephalotes*, *Acromyrmex octospinosus*, *Trachymyrmex urichi*, *Sericomyrmex opacus*, *Apterostigma urichi*, *A. mayri* and *Cyphomyrmex rimosus*). His account of the large species of *Atta* adds little of interest to that of previous authors. On two occasions he found the deälated females of *Acromyrmex octospinosus* "working just as hard and engaged in the same occupation as the neuters, viz: cutting leaves and carrying them to the nest. They all issued from the same nest and therefore could not have been mothers of new colonies." He "also noticed that several females lost their wings in the nest without any marital flight, although a few weeks later the winged ones swarmed out in the usual way on a damp evening."

The nest of *Trachymyrmex urichi* is "excavated in clayey soils and never anywhere else. It consists of one chamber at about the depth of a foot and is never directly under the entrance hole, but always on one side at right angles and about 9 inches away from it. It has a habit of carrying the particles of earth which result from its mining operations a little way from the entrance hole, say about a foot, and deposits them in a small conical heap.... These ants also cultivate a fungus and if it is not *Rozites gongylophora* it is very much like it.... Any roots of plants going through the ants' chamber are not cut away, but are made to suspend their mushroom gardens which are in their case regular hanging gardens.... They are nocturnal in habits and when disturbed sham death." They "seem to like small fallen flowers and the fruit of various kinds of plants to be found in gardens, but at the same time they do not despise rose plants, especially the young and tender shoots. They are not at all energetic and are very slow in their movements."

The habits of *Apterostigma urichi* are described as follows: "Unlike *Atta* this species does not excavate its nests but builds them in rotten trunks of trees.... They are built in hanging position, *i. e.*, the ants start working from the top, but never let the nest touch the bottom of the cavity. Unless the garden is quite recent and small it is always enclosed in a delicate white covering, which at first sight looks like fine cobweb, with an exit hole at the bottom. The nests therefore look like a more or less rounded ball and are never larger than an apple. On breaking away this delicate covering a small mushroom garden is found consisting of irregular cells in which the ants, larvæ and pupæ are scattered." The fungus is similar to that described by Mœller for the Brazilian species of *Apterostigma*. "The gardens are always found under rotten wood and the ants invariably use the excrementa of wood-boring insects as a medium for growing their fungus on. .....The colonies of these ants are small, not numbering more than 20 or 30 dark brown workers, all of about the same size, viz. $6-6\frac{1}{2}$ mm. and with abnormally long legs which measure $7-7\frac{1}{2}$ mm. without the hip. They are of nocturnal habits." The smaller *A. mayri* constructs similar gardens in dark cavities, not only under rotten wood but also under large stones. It, too, collects the excrement of wood-boring insects, but is also fond of fruits or even parts of flowers. The mycelium has the kohlrabi aggregated into regular clusters and according to Urich represents a more advanced condition than that of *A. urichi*. The ants are nocturnal and sham death for many seconds.

Urich has also given us the only existing account of the habits of a *Sericomyrmex* (*S. opacus*). "The nests of these ants are found commonly about Port of Spain, in gardens, in the grass as a rule, but sometimes in the flower beds, and from their peculiar raised entrance can be readily recognized.

They are always excavated in clayey soil, and the raised entrances, which are more or less cylindrical, are constructed with the particles of earth resulting from their mining operations and are about an inch in height.   In young colonies this entrance leads into a small chamber, about six inches below the surface of the ground, situated not at the end of the gallery but either to the left or right of it.   As the colony increases the ants do not enlarge this original chamber, but, piercing its side, form another chamber near it with a small entrance hole.   In large colonies, which never consist of more than about 200 individuals, a nest consists of two or three chambers which open on the original excavation.   This is no longer used for growing the fungus in, but forms a sort of ante-chamber which generally contains material brought in by the ants to grow their mushrooms on, which is deposited here and gradually made use of.   The chambers adjoining are more or less round, with a diameter of about 2–3 inches, and any small roots of plants growing through them are not cut away but used by the ants to hang their mushroom gardens on.   These fill the interior of the chamber and consist of a gray spongy mass consisting of a great number of little irregular cells and resembling a coarse sponge, amongst which are scattered larvæ, pupæ and ants. The walls of the cells consist of small round pellets resembling dust shot and are penetrated by and enveloped in white fungus hyphæ, which hold the mass together.   Strewn thickly upon the surface of the garden are to be seen round white bodies about a quarter of a millimeter in diameter.   These are what Mœller terms "Kohlrabi" clumps, and consist of an aggregation of hyphæ with special swellings at their ends.   It is on this that the ants feed.   The fungus found by Mœller in the nests of the Brazilian fungus growers (*Acromyrmex*) is the *Rozites gongylophora*, Mœller, and if it is not the same species cultivated by *S. opacus* it is, at any rate, very nearly related to it.   As material to grow their mushrooms on the ants make use of particles of fruit, flowers, and leaves, but prefer fruit.   They do well in artificial nests, constructed on Sir John Lubbock's plan, and are easy to watch.   I have tried them with all kinds of vegetable products; they have taken orange, banana, rose petals and leaves and once they even made use of the dried glue from the back of an old book lying near their nest, but that day they had nothing else; if the choice be left to them they invariably take fruit and seem to prefer the orange amongst these.   Very small particles of the white skin of the oranges are torn off, and after undergoing a slight kneading process in the ants' mandibles, are planted in the nest.   The neuters are all of the same size, varying but slightly and never exceed 4 mm. in length. They are more diurnal in their habits than other species of fungus growers,— but also work a little at night.   I have found winged forms in the nests in the month of July."

Urich is responsible for the erroneous statement that *Cyphomyrmex rimosus* "does not cultivate any fungus," a statement which has been repeated by subsequent writers (Forel, Emery).

In 1896 Swingle read a paper on *Trachymyrmex septentrionalis* (= *tardigrada* auct.) before the American Association for the Advancement of Science. He says: "In July of this year I examined some colonies of *Atta tardigrada*, which Mr. Pergande had found in the vicinity of Washington. The nests are small subterranean cavities, 6–10 cm. in diameter, situated from 2 to 15 or 20 cm. below the surface. Some nests have one cavity, others two. Almost the whole cavity is filled with a grayish material loosely and irregularly connected together. By watching the ants, it was determined that they carried into their nests the excrements of some leaf-eating insect, lying on the ground under neighboring oak-trees. The same material was found to constitute at least a large part of the substance filling the nest. Even with a low magnifying lens, tufts of minute sparkling bodies could be seen on the fragments of the fungus garden, while the whole mass was interpenetrated by the white mycelium of a fungus. Examination with higher magnification showed that the glistening tufts were really composed of 'Kohlrabi' even more perfectly spherical than figured by M. Mœller. The mature 'Kohlrabi' were very much larger than the mycelium below, being 22 to 52 μ wide and 30 to 56 μ long, while the supporting mycelial threads were only 4 to 8 μ in diameter. There are no septa dividing the 'Kohlrabis' from the mycelial threads. The whole appearance of the fungus is strikingly similar to that found by Mœller, and it is by no means impossible that it will prove to be the same species though the Kohlrabis are nearly twice as large as what he reports."

Forel (1896*a–c*, 1897, 1899–1900*b*) has recorded a number of observations on the *Attii* of Colombia (*A. sexdens, cephalotes* and *lævigata*; *Acromyrmex octospinosus*, and species of *Trachymyrmex, Sericomyrmex, Mycocepurus*, and *Apterostigma*). He excavated one of the huge nests of *A. sexdens* belonging to an extensive colony at Rio Frio (1896*b*). "This nest looked like an immature volcano and consisted of a mass of 12 to 20 fused craters. The whole nest was 5 or 6 m. in diameter and about 1 m. high. The largest (median) crater was about 60 cm. in diameter, 28 cm. high, and had an opening below of about $3\frac{1}{2}$ cm. The smaller accessory nests in the neighborhood (100 to 200 steps distant) had only 2–3 craters and were much smaller. There are two kinds of craters; one consisting of sand or soil of a gray color and consisting of the excavated earth, the others are brown and consist of the rejected and useless remains of the gardens, *i. e.*, the portions that have been exhausted by the fungi, thrown out in this manner in the form of brown pellets. The medium-sized workers are seen continually coming out of the latter craters laden with brown pellets which they cast aside, while into the gray craters a stream of the same kind of workers is entering in an almost continuous procession laden with green leaves. Some small workers also stand around the openings. On disturbing the nest one is severely attacked by the largest workers. With their sharp jaws, worked by enormous muscles, they can bite so severely as to bring the blood; in fact, a small artery in my little finger was severed by one of these workers. The wounds were as much as 4 mm. in length. Nevertheless Mr. Bradbury, a native and myself attacked the nest with a shovel and dug into it deeply. Thousands of the large workers rushed out at us. The half-naked Indian ran away and I had to retreat from time to time with bleeding hands. But the interior of the nest was laid bare. This consisted of a number of great cavities, 15 to 20 cm. long and 8–12 cm. high and each was nearly always filled with a fungus garden, which looks very much like the single garden of the *Acromyrmex* species. In the labyrinth of this gray to brown garden live thousands of the smallest and medium sized workers, together with the whole ant brood. Colossal female larvæ are there found covered with a regular envelope of larvæ of all sizes, so that they have the appearance of hedge hogs. The workers held fast to the larvæ so tenaciously that I could take them in my hands and even kill them in alcohol without their losing their hold....The large species of *Atta* therefore have not only one but hundreds of fungus gardens. The fungus chambers communicate with one another by means of broad galleries 2–3 cm. in diameter. The lower portion of the garden is uniformly light rust-red with white fungus patches, whereas the upper portions are more gray. The dark brown portions seem to represent the residuum. The fungus garden is so friable that it is impossible to remove it without destroying its form. How the old myth, or nonsense, that these *Atta* species line their nests with leaves could have originated and could even be revamped by McCook is incomprehensible to me....All the pupæ are naked, that is, not enclosed in cocoons. The workers have the habit of carrying their straying sisters exactly like our species of *Formica* (the carried ant is rolled under the head of the carrier)." In another place (1899, 1900*b*) Forel says that *Acromyrmex octospinosus* carries its sister workers in the reverse position, *i. e.*, like *Myrmica*. He also describes (1896*b*) very briefly the nests and distribution of *A. cephalotes* and *lævigata*. The latter also has very large but deeply subterranean nests. It lives more in the mountains at and above an altitude of 1,000 m. and so far down in the ground that Forel could not reach the fungus gardens. *Cephalotes* is intermediate; its nests are nearly as large as those of *sexdens* and the fungus-gardens have a very similar structure and arrangement. The colonies of *cephalotes* and especially of *lævigata*, are less populous than those of *sexdens*. The nests of *cephalotes* occur from sea-level to an altitude of more than 1,000 m., those of *sexdens* only in the low-lying regions.

According to von Ihering (1898) the nest of the Brazilian *Atta sexdens* differs from that of the Colombian form described by Forel. It consists of from one to two dozen chambers, each 25–30 cm. in diameter and 12 to 15 cm. high, with a flat floor and arched ceiling. Each of these chambers, *panellas* (pots) or *pratos* (plates) as they are called by the Brazilians, has one or more, rarely two, galleries entering it at the side and connecting it with the other cavities and the vertical shafts leading to the surface of the nest. The chambers are ½ to 1 m. apart and are excavated at a depth of 4 to 6 m. below the surface or even lower. The fungus gardens are built up on the flat floors of the chambers. Von Ihering found that when the nests are inundated the ants at once remove portions of their fungus gardens to higher ground. When this is impracticable or the inundation is very great, the population of the nest forms a ball held together by the closed jaws of the workers and enclosing in its interior a portion of the fungus garden and probably also the queen. This ball then floats on the water till carried ashore, when the ants land and start a new nest out of reach of the flood. Von Ihering says that his neighbor took advantage of this habit, which by the way is also exhibited by several other tropical ants (*Anomma, Solenopsis geminata*, etc.), to free his premises from the leaf-cutting *Attæ*, by rowing about in his canoe, catching up the floating balls and throwing them into a bucket of boiling water. Von Ihering also gives an interesting account of the *içás*, or virgin queens of *Atta sexdens*. At the time of swarming these are captured in great numbers by the Brazilians. The içá hunter stations himself at the entrance of the nest with his feet in a tub of water in order to protect himself from the savage soldiers and workers, and collects the females while they are issuing from the galleries. A successful catch may yield as many as 12 to 20 litres. The gasters of these içás, removed from the thoraces, legs and heads and roasted with salt, garlic and mandioca meal are eaten as a delicacy ("*passoca*") in many parts of Brazil.

Forel (1899–1900*a*, 1901) has also recorded a few notes on the fungus-gardens of a colony of *Trachymyrmex septentrionalis* which he observed at Black Mountain, North Carolina, but he adds little to the above cited descriptions of Morris, McCook and Swingle. Forel (1905) later published some notes of Gœldi on the nests of *Acromyrmex octospinosus*, the fungus gardens of which are built over the stems of plants and fully exposed to the air in the damp forests of Para. Two photographs accompanying the article show that this fungus garden consists of a number of separate portions unlike the single garden which Urich and Forel describe this ant as making when nesting in the ground.

In 1900 Moreno published some observations on the Mexican *Atta* (probably *fervens*) but these add nothing of value to what was previously known.

In 1901 I recorded a few notes on *Atta fervens* and *Cyphomyrmex rimosus dentatus* which I observed in Mexico. I was able to convince myself that the statements of Urich, Forel and Emery to the effect that the latter species makes no fungus-garden, are erroneous. This ant constructs a fungus garden with caterpillar excrement and cultivates a peculiar fungus consisting of small yellow nodules, which have been overlooked by previous investigators. More recently (1905*a*) I have found that other varieties and subspecies of *C. rimosus* in Texas, Florida, the Bahamas, Porto Rico and Culebra have the same habit. In this same paper I also described briefly the habits of *Trachymyrmex jamaicensis*, and in a subsequent paper (1905*b*) also those of *T. septentrionalis*. A fuller account of these various species will be found in the third part of the present article.

M. T. Cook (1906) has very recently studied the habits of *Atta insularis* and has published a few notes on the ravages of this ant in the plantations of Cuba.

The preceding paragraphs deal almost exclusively with observations on adult colonies of the *Attii* and the constitution and care of their fungus gardens. As soon as these habits had been demonstrated, the question naturally arose as to how the ants first come into possession of the fungi which they cultivate with such marvellous skill and assiduity. The labors of the South American naturalists Sampaio, von Ihering, Gœldi and Jakob Huber have supplied the answer to this interesting question.

Sampaio (1894) on digging up an *Atta* female ten days after the nuptial flight, found her in a cavity with two small white masses, one consisting of 50–60 eggs, the other of a filamentous substance which was the young fungus garden, though not recognized as such. Three and one half months after the nuptial flight he excavated another nest which had an opening to the surface of the soil. He found numerous workers of three different sizes but all smaller than the corresponding castes in adult colonies. They were already cutting leaves and had a fungus garden about 30 cubic centimeters in volume. He estimated the number of workers at 150 to 170, that of the larvæ and pupæ at about 150 and the eggs at 50.

The much more important observations of von Ihering (1898), including his brilliant discovery of the method of transfer of the fungus culture from the maternal to the daughter colony, deserve fuller consideration. According to this observer there are repeated nuptial flights of the Brazilian *Atta sexdens* from the end of October to the middle of December. These flights are essentially like those of other ants. On descending to the earth the fertilized female "rids herself of her easily detached wings by quick motions of her legs and then begins to dig her burrow in some spot more or less free from vegetation. This canal is nearly or quite vertical and measures about 12–15 mm. in diameter. It is so narrow that the 'Iça' cannot turn around in it, but is compelled to walk backwards whenever she returns to the surface. She bites off lumps of earth with her powerful jaws, makes them into a pellet by means of loose threads of saliva, brings them up and deposits them a short distance from the entrance to the burrow. The earth thus brought up forms a circular wall, thickened in front and interrupted behind, about 4–5 cm. broad in front and at that point 3 cm. from the entrance. The burrow varies from 20–30 cm. in length according to circumstances and ends in a small laterally placed chamber about 6 cm. long and somewhat less in height. As soon as the chamber is completed, the ant closes the upper portion of the burrow to a distance of 8–10 cm. from the entrance with pellets of earth and this closure becomes more and more compact in the course of weeks, probably through the action of the rain. If the nest be opened in one or two days, the female will be found in the empty chamber unchanged, only more lethargic, as if exhausted. A few days later one finds near the ant a little packet of 20–30 eggs undergoing segmentation. Beside them lies a flat heap of loose white substance, only 1–2 mm. in diameter. This is the earliest rudiment of the fungus garden. Microscopical examination shows that it consists of compact masses of the well-known fungus-hyphæ, but without traces of "kohlrabi" corpuscles. As time goes on the fungus garden grows rapidly and becomes more voluminous till it reaches a diameter of about 20 cm. It seems to consist of closely aggregated spherules about 1 mm. in diameter. As soon as it has attained this size the transparent pyriform globules bud out, which Mœller called 'kohlrabi' and the ant is seen to eat them frequently, She always keeps close to the fungus garden and in it embeds her eggs. The larger of these soon become larvæ. The eggs are not spun over with fungus hyphæ but have the chorion smooth and shining. Eggs are also found in the interior of the fungus mass, which the ant keeps rearranging and redistributing from time to time. It was easy, for purposes of observation, to transfer the ant to a terrarium. Without excavating anew she remained with her garden on the fresh layer of earth. The garden did not grow, but rather diminished in volume, for it is difficult to imitate the conditions, especially the precise degree of moisture, in which it grows and develops in its cavity. I failed therefore to keep the ant and her garden till the first workers appeared. The time required to accomplish this must be between two and three months. Presumably the last phase of this first brood period is very precarious, since leaves must be brought in to serve as a substratum for the further growth of the fungus garden.

In any event, the development of the garden is in need of further elucidation. According to my investigations, which need fuller confirmation, the organic substratum is provided in the form of malaxated eggs, but perhaps the soil, which is rich in vegetable mould, may itself contain nutrient substances .... As soon as the first workers appear, the colony may be regarded as established and the opening up of the burrow, the enlarging of the first chamber, carrying in of leaves, etc., lead to the well-known conditions of the adult colony.... The preceding description is hardly complete without an answer to the question: Whence come the fungus germs for the establishment of the new garden?" After searching the queen for fungus spores concealed about her person, von Ihering made the important discovery that "every *Atta* queen, on leaving the parental nest, carries in the posterior portion of her oral chamber a loose pellet, .6 mm. in diameter, consisting of hyphæ of *Rozites gongylophora*, small fragments of bleached *i. e.*, chlorophylless leaves, and chitinous bristles. The last are undoubtedly derived from the larvæ undergoing ecdysis in the parental nest." Von Ihering is of the opinion that the female keeps the pellet of hyphæ, etc., in her mouth till she has excavated her chamber and then spits it out where it will serve to kindle the fungus garden of the new colony.

The observations of Gœldi, (Forel 1905, Gœldi 1905 *a* and *b*) are little more than a confirmation of those of von Ihering. He maintains that the fungus is actually grown on some of the malaxated eggs of the *Atta* queen, who would thus be sacrificing a part of her offspring as a culture medium for the fungus that goes to nourish both herself and her workers in their larval and adult stages.

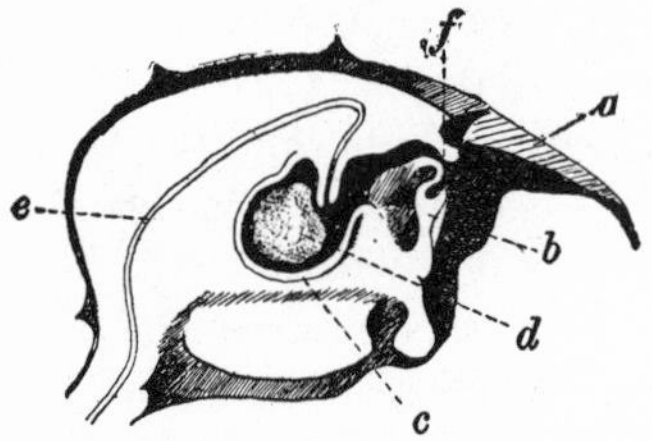

Fig. 1. Head of recently fertilized queen of *Atta sexdens* longitudinally bisected.
a. Mandible; *b*, labium retracted; *c*, buccal pocket containing *d*, the pellet of fungus hyphæ carried from the parental nest; *e*, œsophagus; *f*, oral orifice. (After J. Huber.)

None of these investigators succeeded in rearing an *Atta* colony from its very inception till the hatching of the firstling workers and the bringing in of the leaves for the purpose of keeping up the fungus culture. This has been accomplished very recently by Jakob Huber (1905) who besides correcting a few errors in the work of his predecessors, has added a number of new and important observations. His paper, from which the following abstract is taken, also contains several interesting figures from photographs of the *Atta* female, her progeny, and fungus garden. The female expels the pellet from her buccal pocket (Fig. 1, *c*) the day following the nuptial flight. It is a little mass .5 mm. in diameter, white, yellowish or even black in color, and consists of fungus hyphæ imbedded in the substances collected from the ant's body by means of the strigils on her fore feet and thence deposited in her mouth. By the third day 6 to 10 eggs are laid (Fig. 2). At this time also the pellet begins to send out hyphæ in all directions. The female separates the pellet into two masses on this or the following day (Fig. 3). For the next 10 to 12 days she lays about 10 eggs daily, while the fungus flocculi grow larger and more numerous. At first the eggs and flocculi are kept separate, but they are soon brought together and at least a part of the eggs are placed on or among the flocculi. Eight or ten days later the flocculi have become so numerous that they form when brought together a round or elliptical disc about 1 cm. in diameter. This disc is converted into a dish-like mass with central depression in which the eggs and larvæ are thenceforth kept. The first larvæ appear about 14 to 16 days after the *Atta* female has completed her burrow, and the first pupæ appear about a month after the

Fig. 2.   Eggs and fungus garden in cell of queen *Atta sexdens*, forty-eight hours after the nuptial flight.   (After J. Huber.)

inception of the colony. By this time the fungus garden has a diameter of about 2 cm. There are no "kohlrabi" corpuscles in the earlier stages, and when first seen they are at the periphery of the disc. A week later the pupæ begin to turn brown and in a few days the first workers hatch. Hence the time required for the establishment of a colony under the most favorable conditions is about 40 days. After this rapid survey of the matter, Huber asks the important question: How does the *Atta* female manage to keep the fungus alive? Obviously the small amount of substance in the original pellet must soon be exhausted and the growing hyphæ must be supplied with nutriment from some other source. His interesting answer to this question may be given in his own words: "After carefully watching the ant for hours she will be seen suddenly to tear a little piece of the fungus from the garden

Fig. 3.   Eggs and fungus garden in cell of queen *Atta sexdens* seventy-two hours after the nuptial flight.   (After J. Huber.)

with her mandibles and hold it against the tip of her gaster, which is bent forward for this purpose (Fig. 4). At the same time she emits from her vent a clear yellowish or brownish droplet which is at once absorbed by the tuft of hyphæ. Hereupon the tuft is again inserted, amid much feeling about with the antennæ, in the garden, but usually not in the same spot from which it was taken, and is then patted in place by means of the fore feet (Fig. 5). The fungus then sucks up the drop more or less quickly.

Often several of these drops may be clearly seen scattered over the young fungus garden [Fig. 6]. According to my observations this performance is repeated usually once or twice an hour, and sometimes, indeed, even more frequently. It can almost always be observed a number of times in succession when a mother ant that has no fungus, as sometimes happens in the cultures, is given a piece of fun-

Fig. 4. Silhouette of a queen *Atta sexdens* in the act of manuring her fungus garden. (From an instantaneous photograph after J. Huber.)

gus belonging to another *Atta* female or from an older colony. The mother ant is visibly excited while she explores the gift with her antennæ, and usually in a few minutes begins to divide it up and re-build it. At such times she first applies each piece to her vent in the manner above described and drenches it with a fecal droplet." From these observations Huber concludes that the droplet must be liquid excrement and that the fungus owes its growth to this method of manuring. A direct use of malaxated eggs for this purpose was never observed and could not be detected by microscopical examination, although a number of observations show that the same result may be accomplished indirectly, namely by the female eating her own eggs. This habit is so common and apparently so normal that Huber estimates that 9 out of every 10 eggs are devoured by the mother, often as soon as they are laid. The life of the *Atta* female in her little cell during all this time is very rhythmical. At regular intervals she conscientiously examines the walls of the cavity, flattens out the earth, etc. She devotes more time to licking and manuring the fungus garden and, of course, lavishes most care on the brood. As soon as the larvæ appear they are fed directly with eggs thrust into their mouths by their mother. Huber con-

Fig. 5. Silhouette of a queen *Atta sexdens* replacing in the fungus garden tuft of mycelium saturated with fecal liquid. (From an instantaneous photograph after J. Huber.)

cludes that this is their normal diet till the first workers hatch. He never saw the female either eating the fungus mycelium herself or feeding it to the young. As proof of his contention he cites the case of one of his *Atta* queens who brought up a brood without a fungus garden. With the appearance of the firstling workers, which are minims, that is members of the smallest worker caste, a change comes over the colony. They begin to

usurp the functions of the mother ant.   They manure the garden, which at
the time of their appearance measures hardly more than 2.5 cm. in diameter,
and feed the larvæ with their mothers' eggs.   The workers themselves,
however, feed on the "kohlrabi" which has been developing on the hyphæ
in the meantime.   After about a week some of the workers begin to dig in
the earth, and ten days after the appearance of the first worker and seven
weeks after the inception of the colony, they break through to the surface
of the soil and surround the entrance of the nest with a tiny crater of earthen
pellets.   They now begin to bring in pieces of leaves, knead them up into
minute wads, and insert them in the fungus garden.   The method of man-

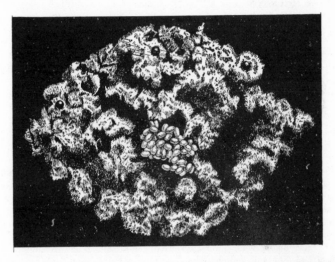

Fig. 6.   Fungus garden of *Atta sexdens* fourteen days after the nuptial flight.   There are
about 100 eggs which the queen has placed in a depression in the middle of the garden.   Near
the periphery there are three drops of the fecal liquid with which the queen manures her garden.
(After J. Huber.)

uring the garden with fecal droplets seems now to be abandoned.   The
mother *Atta* henceforth pays no attention to the development of the garden or
to the brood, but degenerates into a sluggish egg-laying machine, while the
multifarious labors of the colony devolve on the workers.   In the meantime
the "kohlrabi" has become so abundant that it can be fed to the larvæ.   In
concluding his paper Huber makes the important observation that fertile
females of *Atta sexdens* are readily adopted by strange workers of their own
species.   Such adoptions may be frequently resorted to in a state of nature
and would perhaps account for the enormous size and great age of some of
the formicaries of the larger species of *Atta*, which in this respect resemble
the colonies of *Formica rufa* and *F. exsectoides* in the north temperate zone.

PART II. DESCRIPTIONS OF NORTH AMERICAN ATTII.

1. **Atta texana** *Buckley.*

Myrmica (Atta) texana BUCKLEY, Proc. Acad. Nat. Sci. Phila., 1860, p. 233, ☿ ♀ ♂.
Myrmica texana BUCKLEY, Proc. Acad. Nat. Sci. Phila., 1861, pp. 9–10.
Œcodoma texana LINCECUM, Proc. Acad. Nat. Sci. Phila., 1867, pp. 24–31.
Œcodoma texana BUCKLEY, Proc. Ent. Soc. Phila., VI, 1867, p. 347, no. 62, ☿ ♀ ♂.
Atta fervens TOWNSEND, Amer. Entom. and Botan., II, 1870, pp. 324–325, figs. 202
   and 203, ☿ ♀.
Atta fervens McCOOK, Ann. Mag. Nat. Hist., (5) III, 1879, pp. 442–449.
Atta fervens McCOOK, Nature, XX, 1879, p. 583.
Atta fervens McCOOK, Proc. Acad. Nat. Sci. Phila., 1879, pp. 33–40.
Œcodoma texana NEHRLING, Zool. Garten, XXV, 1884, p. 265.
Atta fervens DALLA TORRE, Catalog. Hymen., VII, 1893, pp. 152, 153 (in part).
Atta fervens EMERY, Zool. Jahrb., Abth. f. Syst., VIII, 1894, p. 329.
Atta fervens FOREL, Biol. Centr. Amer., Hymen., III, 1899-1900, p. 33 (in part).
Atta fervens WHEELER, Amer. Natur., XXXV, 1900, pp. 851–862, 2 figs.
Atta fervens WHEELER, Trans. Texas Acad. Sci., IV, no. 2, 1902, p. 13.

Soldier. (Fig. 7 and Pl. XLIX, Fig. 11.)   Length 10–12 mm.
   Head cordate without the mandibles broader than long, with rounded posterior
corners and shallow obtuse occipital excision.   Mandibles long, flattened, with a
large acute apical and 9 or 10 blunt, subequal basal teeth.   Clypeus short and broad,
with bidentate and arcuately excised anterior border.   Frontal carinæ continued
as distinct, diverging ridges as far back as the middle of the head; their lobes with
a prominent tooth above the insertion of each antennal scape.   Frontal area large,
triangular, indistinct.   Antennæ slender.   Eyes convex, hemispherical, about ¼ the
distance from the anterior to the posterior corners of the head.   Ocelli absent.
There is a tooth on the lateral carina between the eye and the clypeus, two small
spines or teeth on the ventrolateral surface of the head, one or two similar teeth on
each occipital lobe and behind them a large prominent spine.   Thorax with four
pairs of spines: one small acute pair on the inferior corners of the pronotum, a
large robust, acute and erect pair, sometimes reduced to conical projections, above
on the sides of the pronotum; a much shorter, often more slender and less tapering
pair on the mesonotum, and a long, acute, backwardly directed pair on the epinotum.
The last are prolonged forward at their bases in the form of a pair of anteriorly converging ridges.   Petiole about 1½ times as long as broad, pentagonal from above,
broadest in the middle; node concave in the middle with a ridge on each side.   Postpetiole nearly twice as broad as the petiole, about as broad as long, narrowed in
front, flattened above, with a pair of more pronounced and uneven mesial and a pair
of shorter and feebler lateral ridges.   Gaster oval, broadest at the middle, with
somewhat angular anterior corners and abruptly conical tip.   Legs very long and
slender.
   Mandibles and clypeus shining; the former coarsely striatopunctate, the latter
finely and unevenly punctate.   Remainder of body opaque, very finely punctate or
granular.
   Hairs long, erect or reclinate, curved, golden yellow or fulvous, covering the

body and appendages.   Pubescence abundant on the body and rather long, of the same color as the hairs; absent on the appendages, with the exception of the antennal funiculi.

Ferruginous brown; borders of mandibles black.

Media.   (Fig. 7 and Pl. XLIX, Fig. 13).   Length: 3-9 mm.

Resembling the soldier but with proportionally smaller head and all the cephalic and thoracic spines longer and more acute, especially the posterior occipital and the superior pronotal pairs.   The latter are often much longer than the epinotal spines and curved forward at their tips.

Minima.   (Fig. 7 and Pl. XLIX, Fig. 14.)   Length: 1.5-2.5 mm.

Head proportionally smaller than in the soldier and media; mandibular teeth more acute; lobes of frontal carinæ, lateral carinæ and ventro-lateral surfaces of head without teeth.   Anterior and posterior occipital spines much reduced.   On the thorax the superior are not longer than the inferior pronotal spines and much shorter than those on the epinotum.   Pubescence and hairs much sparser and more inconspicuous than in the soldier and media.

Female.   (Fig. 7.)   Length: 17-18 mm.

Head without the mandibles, much broader than long, arcuately excised behind, with rather straight, anteriorly converging sides.   Mandibles and clypeus similar to those of the soldier, but the former with at least 12 basal teeth, the latter with the two teeth of its anterior border blunter and more prominent.   Frontal and lateral carinæ with prominent teeth.   Spines of anterior occipital and ventro-lateral surface of head reduced to low projections.   Posterior occipital spines small but acute. Thorax robust, distinctly longer than the first gastric segment; twice as broad as the head.   Inferior pronotal spines small and acute; superior pair lacking.   Scutellum rounded, convex, without a median longitudinal impression.   Epinotum with a pair of small, acute, backwardly directed spines, each of which has a prominent, elongate swelling in front of its base.   Petiole more than twice as broad as long; broadest in the middle and produced on each side into a long, slender spine or process.   Postpetiole less than twice as broad as the petiole and fully twice as broad as long, widest behind with two pairs of truncated lateral projections, of which the posterior is the longer.   Lower surface with a prominent transverse ridge.   Gaster nearly as broad as long, but little broader in the middle than at its straight anterior border.   Anterior corners of first segment rectangular.   Legs slender and weak.

Mandibles, anterior border of clypeus, scapes and legs shining; clypeus and mandibles punctate, the latter also very coarsely striated.   Remainder of body opaque, granular-rugulose.   Mesopleuræ coarsely rugose.

Hairs and pubescence tawny, the former dense and erect on the body and appendages, the latter sparse, somewhat reclinate and hooked, most conspicuous on the head and gaster.

Deep maroon brown, legs more reddish; borders of mandibles black.   Wings with ferruginous brown veins and a strong suffusion of the same color in the membranes, especially along their anterior borders.

Male.   (Fig. 7, and Pl. XLIX, Fig. 24.)   Length: 13-14 mm.

Head small, without the mandibles but little broader than long, flattened behind but not excised, with large and very prominent eyes and ocelli.   Mandibles well-developed, with pointed tips and about a dozen blunt basal teeth. Anterior border of clypeus with two broad blunt teeth and a median excision. Space between frontal and lateral carinæ concave, elliptical. Antennæ slender. Cephalic spines obsolete, except those of the posterior occipital region, which are short, acute and sometimes bent downwards at their tips. Thorax through the wing insertions more than twice as broad as the head. Mesonotum as broad as long, projecting in front over the small pronotum, which has a short, broad tooth at its inferior corner on each side. Scutellum convex, with a faint longitudinal impression in the middle. Epinotum unarmed. Petiole and postpetiole similar to those of the female, but each side of the former sometimes with two spines of unequal length, and the postpetiole is less angular on the sides. Gaster as broad as long, elliptical, convex above and below. Hypopygium broader than long, fenestrate, with its free edge faintly bidentate and not excised but instead slightly produced in the middle. Outer genital appendages slender, strap-shaped with subparallel borders and obliquely truncated tips. Median pair long with infolded edges and geniculate towards the apex, which is flattened and provided with a strong basal and two feebler terminal teeth. Wings 22 mm. long.

Mandibles somewhat shining, finely striate and coarsely punctate. Head and thorax opaque, pedicel and gaster slightly shining. Clypeus, frontal area and facial concavities uniformly granular, remainder of head coarsely reticulate-rugose. Thorax rather coarsely granular and punctate. Mesonotum with undulating transverse rugulæ. Pedicel and gaster densely and finely punctate, with more scattered, larger piligerous punctures. Legs and genitalia shining.

Hairs fulvous brown, long, dense, and erect on the head and upper portions of thorax and pedicel, sparser on the pleuræ and legs; on the gaster much shorter and sparser and hardly more than a dilute, suberect pubescence. Outer genital valves and free edge of hypopygium with numerous hairs.

Ferruginous brown; gaster, genitalia, legs and antennæ somewhat paler. Wings like those of the female.

Texas: Chapel Hill, Brenham, La Grange, Ye Gua Creek (Lincecum); Austin (Buckley, Lincecum, Townsend, McCook, Wheeler); Alice, New Braunfels, Elgin, Granite Mountain (Wheeler).

There exists some confusion in the literature in regard to this species. The European myrmecologists, Mayr, Forel and Emery, have confounded it with a closely related, but in my opinion, perfectly distinct Mexican species, *A. mexicana* F. Smith (*A. fervens* Say). The soldiers and mediæ of the latter, of which I possess specimens from Guadalajara (J. F. McClendon), Irapuato (C. H. T. Townsend), Esquinapa (J. H. Batty), Cuernavaca and Queretaro (Wheeler), differ from the corresponding phases of *texana* in having the head smooth, shining and hairless above. In the male the hypopygium (Pl. L, Fig. 25) is shorter, distinctly excised in the middle with the blunt teeth further apart, and without a median fenestra. The outer genital appendages are slender and taper to a sharp point; the middle pair are more slender and flattened, less geniculate and more uniformly curved. In Pl. L, Figs. 21–25 are given camera drawings of the male hypopygia of all the species of *Atta* s. str. except *columbica* (which is probably a variety of *cephalotes*), because, as Mayr has shown in his work on the Formicidæ of the Novara Expedition, this scelerite and the genital append-ages furnish excellent characters for distinguishing the species.

2. **Atta mexicana** (*F. Smith*).

The name of this species, which is not known to occur in Texas, though it is widely distributed in Mexico at an altitude of 5,000 to 7,000 feet, must either be attributed to Drury, and not, as has usually been done, to Say, or if, as Dalla Torre maintains, the *Formica fervens* of Drury is merely a syn-onym of *A. cephalotes*, we must adopt *A. mexicana* F. Smith as the name of the Mexican form.   As it seems to me to be impossible to determine the species to which Drury's female specimen belonged, I believe that the name *mexicana* should be adopted.   The synonymy disentangled from that of *A. texana* would then read as follows:

? *Formica fervens* DRURY, Illustr. Nat. Hist., III, 1782, p. 58, pl. 42, fig. 3.   ♀.

Atta fervens SAY, Boston Journ. Nat. Hist., I, 3, 1836, p. 290, ♀.

Œcodoma mexicana F. SMITH, Catalog. Hymen. Brit. Mus., VI, 1858, p. 185, no. 9 ♀. Pl. X, fig. 20.

Œcodoma Mexicana NORTON, Amer. Natur., II, 1868, p. 66, pl. I, figs. 9 and 10. ☿ ♀.

Œcodoma mexicana NORTON, Proc. Essex Inst., VI, 1868, Comm. p. 9, fig. ☿ ♀.

? *Œcodoma mexicana* MORENO, Naturaleza, III, 1876, pp. 189–190.

Atta fervens LECONTE, Writings of Th. Say., Entom., II, 1859, p. 734.

Atta fervens MAYR, Reise der Novara, II, 1. Formicidæ, 1865, p. 81, ☿ ♀ ♂.

Atta fervens FOREL, Bull. Soc. Vaud. Sc. Nat., XX, 1884, p. 47 (in part).

Atta fervens DALLA TORRE, Catalog. Hymen., VII, 1893, pp. 152, 153 (in part).

Atta lævigata PERGANDE, Proc. Calif. Acad. Nat. Sci. (2), V, 1895, p. 896, ☿.

Atta fervens FOREL, Biol. Centr.–Am., Hymen., III, 1899–1900, p. 33 (in part).

Atta fervens FOREL, Ann. Soc. Ent. Belg., XLV, 1901, p. 124, ☿.

Atta fervens WHEELER, Ann. Soc. Ent. Belg., XLV, 1901, p. 200, ☿.

3. **Atta (Mœllerius) versicolor** *Pergande.*

Atta versicolor PERGANDE, Proc. Calif. Acad. Sci. (2), IV, 1893, pp. 31, 32, ☿.

Atta (Acromyrmex) versicolor EMERY, Zool. Jahrb., Abth. f. Syst., VIII, 1894, p. 330, ☿.

Atta versicolor FENNER, Entom. News, VI, 1895, p. 215.

Atta (Acromyrmex) versicolor FOREL, Biol. Centr.-Am., Hymen., III, 1899–1900, p. 36, ☿.

Atta (Mœllerius) versicolor EMERY. R. Accad. Sci. Ist. Bologna, April 1905, pp. 108, 111, ☿.

Worker, (Pl. XLIX, Fig. 5.) Length: 2.3–6 mm.

Head without the mandibles broader than long, in larger specimens somewhat narrowed in front, broadly and obtusely excised behind, with rounded posterior corners and slightly convex sides. Eyes convex, less than $\frac{1}{3}$ the distance from the anterior to the posterior corners. Mandibles rather convex, with several blunt teeth. Clypeus concave in the middle, with two very short, blunt teeth on the anterior margin. Frontal carinæ with expanded, toothed lobes in front. Frontal area obsolete. Antennal scapes reaching to the posterior corners of the head, somewhat incrassated towards their tips. Lateral carinæ with a short, acute tooth. Postocular spines absent; anterior and superior occipital regions with a number of short teeth or spines; posterior occipital region with a longer acute spine on each side. Pronotum with a pair of short, downwardly directed inferior and a pair of long, robust and acute superior spines directed forward and outward. Mesonotum with two pairs of spines, the anterior about half as long as the superior pronotal pair, but more rapidly tapering and directed upward and backward; the posterior pair smaller and closer together. Epinotum with two spines which are nearly as long as the superior pronotal pair but more slender and directed backward, upward and slightly outward. Petiole longer than broad, its node subrectangular, with four equidistant, subequal teeth in a transverse row. Postpetiole nearly twice as broad as the petiole, broader than long, concave above, with six short bidentate spines, four in a transverse anterior row and two behind and more widely separated at their bases. Gaster broadly elliptical, broadest behind the middle; basal segment with a median longitudinal depression, on each side of which there are several acute tubercles, longest near the anterior and lateral margins.

Mandibles shining, coarsely punctate and striate; remainder of body, including the legs and scapes, opaque, densely punctate. Head, thorax, pedicel and anterior border of gaster vermiculately or reticulately rugulose. Basal gastric segment with scattered, shallow foveolæ.

Hairs brown or tawny, suberect, not very abundant, rather short, curved or hooked on the body, straighter on the scapes and legs.

Ferruginous brown; borders of mandibles and anterior border of clypeus black.

Female. Length: 8 mm.

Head resembling that of the worker, but the posterior corners are more acute and the antennal scapes are longer. Pronotum with two broad and rather blunt inferior and two acute superior spines, which are directed forward and outward. Scutellum trapezoidal with bidentate posterior edge. Epinotal spines long, curved and diverging, of nearly uniform thickness up to their rapidly tapering tips which are bent downwards. Petiole and postpetiole similar to those of the worker, but the median pair of teeth in the former longer than the lateral pair and the spines on the postpetiole reduced to small teeth. Gaster pyriform, with the first segment flattened above and without the pointed tubercles.

Mandibles and legs shining; remainder of body opaque. Head coarsely, densely and crenately rugose, the rugæ being longitudinal on the sides but diverging from the front and median line on the upper surface. Thorax covered with rugæ similar to those on the head, transverse on the pronotum, longitudinal on the mesonotum and pleuræ, and irregular on the scutellum. Pedicel and gaster densely and irregularly rugulose; on the middle of the first segment of the latter the rugulæ are more regular and longitudinal. Antennal scapes and legs coarsely punctate and more or less roughened.

Pilosity like that of the worker.

Ferruginous brown; upper surface of head, mesonotum and gaster blackish, the mesonotum with a V-shaped red spot on the middle and the gaster with a pair of elliptical ferruginous spots on the basal segment. Wings opaque yellowish brown, with dull yellow veins.

Male. (Pl. L, Fig. 26.) Length: 8 mm.

Head, without the mandibles and eyes, as long as broad, subrectangular, with nearly straight posterior border. Eyes large, protruding, hemispherical, with their posterior orbits at the middle of the head. Mandibles well-developed, acute, flattened and multidentate. Clypeus very faintly and sinuately excised in the middle. Frontal and lateral carinæ without teeth. Antennal scapes extending fully ⅓ their length beyond the posterior corners of the head. The latter with a small, acute superior and a broad flattened inferior tooth on each side. Pronotum with a larger inferior and much smaller superior tooth on each side. Mesonotum with distinct Mayrian furrows. Scutellum with a median longitudinal depression and a pair of blunt posterior teeth. Epinotum with short, convex base and longer straight declivity; spines like those of the female but more slender and tapering more gradually. Petiole and postpetiole like those of the female, the former with small acute teeth above and three lateral teeth, the latter with four teeth on each side. Gaster broadly elliptical, with the basal segment flattened above and without tubercles. Genital appendages convex, curved inward, with broad, rounded, subtruncate tips. Legs slender.

Body including the mandibles and legs, opaque; gaster slightly shining. Mandibles finely striated and coarsely punctate. Head, thorax and pedicel densely rugulose, the rugulæ being longitudinal on the head, mesonotum, scutellum, pleuræ and epinotum, and transverse on the pronotum, petiole and postpetiole. Gaster and legs densely punctate. Genital appendages with a few scattered foveolæ.

Pilosity like that of the worker and female.

Black; mandibles, border of clypeus, frontal carinæ, neck, antennæ, coxæ, tibiæ, tarsi and gaster ferruginous brown, posterior borders of gastric segments and genitalia somewhat paler. Wings like those of the female.

Arizona: Tucson (Fenner, Wheeler); Yucca (Wheeler).

Mexico: Calamujuet, Lower California (Eisen and Haines); Sonora (Coll. Am. Mus. Nat. Hist.).

The types are from Calamujuet; the above description is drawn from Tucson specimens.

4. Atta (Mœllerius) versicolor chisosensis subsp. nov.

A number of workers taken by Judge O. W. Williams in the Chisos Mountains of southwestern Texas, and a few workers taken by myself at Terlingua in the same region, represent a distinct subspecies.

They differ from the typical *versicolor* in their distinctly lighter and more yellowish color, much less pronounced sculpture and in having only a few (about 12) pointed tubercles on each side of the median gastric depression, whereas in the typical form there are two or three times as many. Owing to their feebler sculpture the workers of *chisosensis* are throughout much more shining than the typical form.

5. Atta (Trachymyrmex) septentrionalis *McCook*.

? *Œcodoma virginiana* BUCKLEY, Proc. Ent. Soc. Phila., VI, 1867, p. 346, no. 61, ☿.
? *Œcodoma tardigrada* BUCKLEY, Proc. Ent. Soc. Phila., VI, 1867, p. 349, no. 65, ☿.
   ♀ ♂.
Atta septentrionalis McCOOK, Proc. Acad. Nat. Sci. Phila., 1880, pp. 359–363, Fig. ☿.
Atta (Acromyrmex) tardigrada FOREL, Bull. Soc. Vaud. Sci. Nat. (2) XX, p. 91, 1884,
   p. 358, ☿ ♀ ♂.
Atta tardigrada MAYR, Verh. zool. bot. Ges. Wien, XXXVI, 1886, p. 442.
Atta (Trachymyrmex) tardigrada FOREL, Ann. Soc. Ent. Belg., XXXVII, 1893, p.
   601.
Atta tardigrada DALLA TORRE, Catalog. Hymen., VII, 1893, p. 154.
Atta tardigrada var. *septentrionalis*, Catalog. Hymen., VII, 1893, p. 154.
Atta (Trachymyrmex) tardigrada EMERY, Zool. Jahrb., Abth. f. Syst., VIII, 1894,
   p. 329.
Atta (Trachymyrmex) tardigrada FOREL, Rivista Sci. Biol., II, 1900, p. 9.
Atta (Trachymyrmex) tardigrada FOREL, Ann. Soc. Ent. Belg., XLV, pp. 396, 397.
Atta (Trachymyrmex) septentrionalis WHEELER, Trans. Tex. Acad. Sci., IV, Pt. II,
   no. 2, 1902, pp. 13, 14.
Atta (Trachymyrmex) septentrionalis WHEELER, Psyche, June, 1903, p. 101, Fig.
   6b.
Atta (Trachymyrmex) septentrionalis WHEELER, Bull. Am. Mus. Nat. Hist., XXI,
   1905, pp. 386, 387.

Worker. (Pl. XLIX, Fig. 4.) Length: 2.5–3 mm.

Head, without the mandibles, about as broad as long, a little broader behind than in front, with obtusely excised posterior border, somewhat rounded posterior angles and rather straight sides. Eyes not very prominent, more than $\frac{1}{3}$ the distance from the anterior to the posterior corners of the head. Mandibles with two larger acute apical and 7 or 8 small basal teeth. Anterior border of clypeus sinuately excised in the middle. Frontal area triangular, obsolescent. Frontal carinæ with flattened, rounded lobes in front, continued back as a pair of diverging ridges beyond the middle of the head as far as but not meeting the lateral carinæ. Antennal scapes extending about $\frac{1}{4}$ their length beyond the posterior corners of the head, somewhat thickened towards their tips. Region between the frontal carinæ and posterior corners of the head covered with small acute tubercles, one pair of which on the posterior corners is longer and bidentate. Pronotum with a pair of blunt, downwardly directed inferior spines, two long acute superior spines and between these in the middle a pair of short bidentate spines or tubercles, which are closer to each other than to the lateral tubercles. Mesonotum with two pairs of blunt spines. Mesoëpinotal constriction pronounced. Epinotum with four longitudinal rows of tubercles, the inner continued back into the bases of a pair of acute spines which are directed upward, backward and outward and are from $\frac{1}{3}$ to $\frac{1}{2}$ as long as the slightly convex base of the epinotum. Declivity sloping, forming in profile an obtuse angle with the base. The upper surface of the thorax and all the spines, with the exception of the inferior pronotal pair are covered with small tubercles. Petiolar node from above nearly square, a little broader than long; in profile its anterior surface is flattened, its summit acute and furnished with a pair of teeth. On each side of these there is also a small blunt tooth. Postpetiole about as broad as the epinotum, somewhat more than twice as broad as the petiole, and distinctly broader than long, subpentagonal from above, concave in the middle behind and covered with small tubercles. Gaster pyriform, broadest behind the middle; first segment with a faint, longitudinal, median depression and a short ridge on each lateral border. The dorsal surface is covered rather uniformly with small, acute tubercles, as are also the antennal scapes.

Mandibles and anterior border of clypeus faintly shining or glossy, the former finely and densely striated. Remainder of body and appendages opaque and indistinctly granular.

Hairs brownish yellow, short, hooked, more or less erect and not very abundant, usually arising from the small tubercles and covering the body and appendages rather uniformly.

Body ferruginous brown, legs slightly paler, mandibular teeth black, front and vertex dark brown; gaster in many specimens with a broad longitudinal fuscous or blackish stripe on the middle of the first segment.

Female. Length: 3.8–4 mm.

Head resembling that of the worker. Pronotum besides the blunt, downwardly directed inferior spines, with a pair of strong, somewhat flattened, acute superior spines directed outward and somewhat forward. Scutellum semicircularly excised and bidentate behind. Epinotal spines long, of rather uniform thickness to within a short distance of their acute, rapidly tapering tips. Pedicel and gaster as in the worker, but the lateral teeth of the petiole are smaller and blunter and the posterior margin of the postpetiole is excised. Wings 4 mm. long.

Sculpture similar to that of the worker; mesonotum and scutellum covered with rows of small elongated tubercles.

Like the worker also in pilosity and coloration. Head with a large black spot on the ocellar region and the gastric stripe is deeper and more distinct, but not reaching the anterior border of the basal segment. Wings blackish with veins of the same color; costal cell yellowish.

Male. Length: 3–3.5 mm.

Head but little broader behind than in front, broadest in the region of the eyes, with slightly convex posterior border. Eyes convex, posterior orbits at the middle of the head. Mandibles like those of the worker but smaller. Clypeus with broad, entire anterior margin. Frontal carinæ lobed in front, uniting behind with the lateral carinæ, which are furnished with a small tooth in the middle. Posterior corners of head with several small, acute spines or teeth. Antennæ slender; scapes somewhat thickened distally and surpassing the posterior corners by about ⅓ of their length. Pronotum with small acute superior and inferior teeth. Mesonotum with well-developed Mayrian furrows. Scutellum similar to that of the female. Epinotum with subequal base and declivity; spines slender, acute, diverging, bent downward at their tips, their bases continued forward as a pair of crenated ridges on to the base of the epinotum. Petiole and postpetiole like those of the worker, but the latter segment without distinct tubercles. Gaster elliptical, convex above, the first segment with smaller and more scattered tubercles than in the worker and female, and without a median longitudinal impression. Outer genital appendages broad and short, with rounded edges; median pair with straight, slender, pointed tips. Hypopygium entire, with a broad, rounded point in the middle. Legs long and slender; terminal tarsal joint not enlarged.

Opaque, mandibles and clypeus granular; head and thoracic dorsum coarsely, pleuræ, petiole and postpetiole more finely reticulate-rugose. Epinotum and gaster finely reticulate or granular. Legs smoother and somewhat shining.

Pilosity similar to that of the worker and female.

Ferruginous brown; upper surface of head, thorax, pedicel and first gastric segment more or less blackened; legs and posterior borders of gastric segments yellowish; antennal scapes dark brown. Wings as in the female.

Texas: Austin, Montopolis, Milano (Wheeler); Denton (W. H. Long); Paris (Miss A. Rucker, C. T. Brues).

Florida: (Mrs. Mary Treat, T. Pergande), Miami and Jacksonville (Wheeler).

District of Columbia: Washington (Pergande, Swingle).

North Carolina: Black Mountain (Forel).

New Jersey: Vineland (Mrs. Treat); Toms River (Morris, McCook); Lakehurst (Wheeler, W. T. Davis); Lucaston (E. Daecke); Miltown and Manusquam (Davis).

I believe that Buckley's name *tardigrada*, which has been very generally applied to this species, should be rejected and replaced by McCook's *septentrionalis*, first, because Buckley's description will apply equally well to this or the following species or even to *Mycetosoritis hartmanni*, although his account of the nests applies to none of these but rather to a small colony of *Atta texana*; and second, although Forel wrote in 1884 that Mayr had in his possession a type specimen of Buckley's *tardigrada* which made it possible to refer Florida specimens received from Mrs. Treat to this species, Dr. Mayr writes me (March 24, 1902); "Ich besitze von *Atta (Trachymyrmex) tardigrada* keinen Buckley'schen Typus." There is no possible means of ascertaining just what species Buckley described. McCook's description is equally worthless, but his specimens were redescribed by Forel, so that the name *septentrionalis* must stand. The above description is drawn from specimens taken early in May from a single colony at Montopolis, near Austin, Texas. Forel regarded McCook's specimens as representing a variety of the southern form, but Emery failed to distinguish any varietal differences between southern and northern specimens. A number of workers taken by me at Lakehurst, New Jersey are larger (3.4–3.6 mm.) than specimens from Texas and Florida and are of a paler, more yellowish color with a darker and more distinct gastric stripe. A deälated female from Lakehurst and a winged individual from Lucaston, New Jersey agree in having a dark spot on the middle of the pronotum, one on the postpetiole and in having the infuscation of the head and middle of the gaster more extensive. If we regard the New Jersey specimens as representing the typical form of the species it will be necessary to distinguish the darker southern form as a variety, for which I would suggest the name *obscurior* var. nov.

6. Atta (**Trachymyrmex**) turrifex *Wheeler.*

WHEELER, Psyche, June, 1903, pp. 100–102, fig. 6a, ☿ ♀.

Worker. (Pl. XLIX, Fig. 3.) Length: 3–3.75 mm.

Head without the mandibles a little longer than broad, slightly broader behind than in front, with obtusely excised posterior border, rather straight sides and prominent posterior angles. Eyes convex, in front of the middle of the head. Mandibles pointed, 7–8-toothed. Clypeus sinuately and rather deeply excised in the middle. Frontal area triangular, indistinct. Frontal carinæ with large round anterior lobes, somewhat concave in the middle, and continued back as a pair of diverging ridges nearly as far as the posterior corners of the head, but not meeting the almost equally long lateral carinæ. Antennæ robust; scapes reaching only to the posterior corners and fitting into deep grooves between the frontal and lateral carinæ. Upper surface of head, with the exception of these grooves, covered with tubercles, two pairs of which on the superior and inferior portions of the occipital corners are larger than the others and bidentate. Scapes covered with similar but smaller tubercles. Pronotum on each side with an acute downwardly directed inferior spine; above with a pair of rather long, acute lateral spines and a shorter bifurcated median spine. Mesonotum with two pairs of thick blunt spines. Mesoëpinotal constriction very pronounced. Epinotum with subequal base and declivity at right angles to each other in profile; the former convex, the latter concave; spines acute, nearly as long as the base, directed upward, backward and outward and prolonged forward at their bases as a pair of subparallel, crenated ridges lying between a shorter pair of similar lateral ridges. All the thoracic spines, with the exception of the inferior pronotal pair, are covered with small tubercles. Similar tubercles are also scattered over the dorsal surface of the thorax between the spines. Petiole from above as broad as long, nearly square, with a transverse row of four equidistant tubercles across its middle and connected with the median pair by longitudinal ridges. There is another pair near the posterior edge of the segment. Postpetiole twice as broad as the petiole and nearly twice as broad as long, impressed in the middle behind and covered with small tubercles. Gaster suboblong, with straight anterior border and subparallel sides, a little broader behind than in front, convex above and below; first segment with longitudinal ridges half way down its sides, a faint median and two lateral depressions. Its whole surface is covered with small tubercles which are connected with one another by a net-work of indistinct ridges. Legs stout, and as far as the second tarsal joint, covered with tubercles which are somewhat smaller than those on the body.

Mandibles with shining, coarsely striatopunctate tips, and opaque, finely striated bases. Remainder of body opaque, obscurely granular and more or less rugulose.

Hairs brown, hooked, suberect, covering the body and appendages, except the antennal funiculi which are clothed with a very fine whitish pubescence.

Ferruginous brown; front and vertex dark brown, legs somewhat paler than the body. In old specimens the body is darker in color and the roughened portions are overlaid with a bluish bloom.

Female. Length: 4–4.5 mm.

Head resembling that of the worker. Pronotum with short, acute inferior and superior spines, the latter not flattened. Scutellum with two long, blunt teeth and a deep median excision in its posterior border. Base of epinotum barely half as long as the declivity, which is concave; spines long, stout and rather blunt. Pedicel and gaster similar to those of the worker; posterior border of the postpetiole entire. Wings 6 mm. long.

Sculpture similar to that of the worker. Mesonotum and scutellum with indistinct longitudinal rows of small tubercles; remainder of thorax granular, with minute, scattered tubercles.

Pilosity and color like those of the worker. Wings opaque brown, with darker veins.

Texas: Austin, Montopolis, Marble Falls, Fort Stockton, Paisano Pass, Marfa, Del Rio, Langtry (Wheeler).

The worker of this species may be readily distinguished from that of *septentrionalis* by the more pointed posterior corners of the head, the much shorter antennal scapes which do not extend beyond the posterior corners, the unpaired pronotal spine, and the rougher legs and gaster. The female *turrifex* is distinguished by several of these characters and also by the much longer and paler wings.

7. **Atta** (**Trachymyrmex**) **arizonensis** sp. nov.

Female (deälated). (Pl. XLIX, Figs. 9 and 10.) Length: 4.75 mm.

Head, without the mandibles, as broad as long, somewhat broader behind than in front, with straight sides, obtusely excised posterior margin and rather pointed posterior corners. Eyes moderately convex, in front of the middle of the sides. Mandibles with two larger apical and several smaller basal teeth. Anterior border of clypeus sinuately notched in the middle. Frontal area triangular, indistinct. Frontal carinæ with large reflected and rather angular lobes, without rounded impressions in their surfaces, continued back as diverging ridges nearly to the posterior corners of the head, but not meeting the much shorter lateral carinæ. Antennal scapes distally enlarged, extending about ¼ their length beyond the posterior corners of the head. The latter with numerous conical tubercles, two of which on the inferior occipital angles are somewhat larger than the others and double. Pronotum with two small, flat, lappet-like inferior spines and a pair of long, but not compressed superior spines, directed outward and slightly forward. Posterior border of scutellum with a broad median excision and a pair of blunt teeth. Base of epinotum sloping, about half as long as the concave declivity. Spines short, acute, a little longer than broad at the base, directed backward and outward. All the spines of the thorax, excepting the inferior pronotal pair, covered with tubercles.   Petiole from above oblong, slightly longer than broad, with bidentate anterior angles, and a pair of longitudinal dorsal ridges elevated into short spines or teeth at their anterior ends.   Postpetiole more than twice as broad as the petiole, somewhat broader than long, transversely elliptical, with the sides produced in the middle in the form of short double spines; posterior margin semicircularly excised and somewhat reflected; upper surface with a pair of irregular elevations and numerous small tubercles. Gaster subspherical, but little longer than broad, anterior border straight, first segment obtusely ridged on the sides anteriorly, without a median depression and uniformly covered with small tubercles which are somewhat larger on the dorsal than on the ventral side.   Legs well-developed and, like the antennal scapes, covered with small tubercles.

Mandibles somewhat shining, finely striated at their bases, more coarsely towards the inner edges of the blades.   Remainder of body opaque, granulate-rugulose; rugulæ on the sides of the head and between the lateral and frontal carinæ longitudinal and minutely and irregularly tuberculate, on the front converging from each side towards the median line.   On the thorax the rugulæ are irregularly longitudinal, more regularly on the mesonotum and scutellum where they are interrupted by low tubercles.   Postpetiole and first gastric segment, especially at its base, obscurely and longitudinally rugulose.

Hairs dark brown, short, hooked or curved, suberect, uniformly covering the body and appendages.   Antennal funiculi with very fine whitish pubescence.

Ferruginous brown, front and vertex darker, mandibular teeth black.   Whole surface of body bluish pruinose.

Male. Length: 4.5 mm.

Head, without the eyes, somewhat longer than broad, a little broader behind than in front, with straight posterior border.   Posterior orbits at the middle of the head.   Mandibles well-developed, with two larger, acute apical and several small basal teeth.   Clypeus with entire, broadly rounded anterior border.   Frontal carinæ with well-developed anterior lobes and short posterior ridges which bend around laterally and pass over into the lateral carinæ, thus enclosing two elliptical facial cavities.   Antennæ slender, scapes slightly thickened distally and reaching more than ⅓ their length beyond the posterior corners of the head.   Posterior corners with short, acute spines, those on the superior and inferior angles being somewhat larger than the others.   Inferior and superior pronotal spines very small and acute. Mayrian furrows of mesonotum distinct but shallow.   Scutellum like that of the female.   Epinotum with base somewhat shorter than the oblique declivity; spines rather short, somewhat longer than broad at the base, as long as the base of the epinotum, acute, directed backward and slightly outward, covered with small tubercles. Petiole similar to that of the female but concave in the middle and traversed by four longitudinal tuberculate ridges.   Postpetiole less than twice as broad as the petiole, and nearly twice as broad as long, subpentagonal, with broadly excised posterior border and covered with tubercles.   Gaster elliptical, convex above, covered uniformly with small acute tubercles except in the middle line near the base.   Outer genital valves short and broad, with rounded tips; median pair terminating in a straight, attenuate point.   Hypopygium entire, very bluntly pointed in the middle. Legs long and slender, covered with very small and rather indistinct tubercles.   Last tarsal joints enlarged.

Mandibles subopaque, very finely and indistinctly striated. Body and appendages opaque. Facial cavities granular; dorsal portions of head, mesonotum, paraptera and scutellum coarsely and reticulately rugose. Remainder of body coarsely granular, the pronotum, pleuræ and epinotum also more or less irregularly rugulose.

Hairs fulvous, similar to those of the female.

Black or dark brown; mandibles, clypeus, anterior corners of head, funiculi, thoracic sutures, tarsi, knees and tips of tibiæ, genitalia and posterior and lateral borders of the gastric segments fulvous. Wings blackish, with yellowish costal cell and brown veins.

Arizona: Palmerlee, Cochise County, Aug. 24 (C. Schaeffer).

Described from a single female and six males.

This species is clearly distinct though in certain respects it is intermediate between *T. septentrionalis* and *turrifex*. The female differs from that of *turrifex* in the longer antennal scapes, which surpass the posterior corners of the head, and the posteriorly excised postpetiole, and from both this and *septentrionalis* in its much heavier sculpture, the greater size of the pronotal spines and the shape of the gaster, which is not oblong and impressed in the middle.

8. **Atta (Trachymyrmex) jamaicensis** *Ern. André.*

Atta (Acromyrmex) jamaicensis ERN. ANDRÉ, Rev. d'Entom., Juillet, 1893, p. 149, ♀.

Trachymyrmex sharpii FOREL, Trans. Ent. Soc. London, 1893, Pt. IV, Dec. pp. 372, 373, ♀.

Atta (Trachymyrmex) maritima WHEELER, Bull. Am. Mus. Nat. Hist., XXI, 1905, pp. 107–109, pl. vii, figs. 7 and 8, ♀.

Worker. Length: 3.5–4.5 mm.

Head, without the mandibles, as broad as long, somewhat broader behind than in front, with obtusely excised posterior border, rather acute posterior angles and slightly convex sides. Eyes somewhat flattened, in front of the middle of the head. Clypeus with a small sinuate notch in the middle of its anterior border. Frontal area triangular, indistinct. Frontal carinæ with broad subtriangular lobes in front, their surfaces not impressed in the middle, continued back as a pair of diverging ridges to the posterior corners where they meet the postorbital ridges thus enclosing elongated grooves for the antennal scapes. Vertex with a pair of blunt projections and short rows of small tubercles. Each posterior corner of the head with three short blunt spines at the angles of an equilateral triangle. Antennæ slender, scapes somewhat enlarged towards their tips which surpass by less than ⅓ their length the posterior corners. Pronotum with a blunt, lappet-shaped inferior and a long pointed superior spine on each side. In the middle between the two spines is a small double tubercle. Mesonotum with a pair of robust and rather blunt anterior and a pair of small acute posterior spines. Mesoëpinotal constriction long and rather shallow. Epinotum with subequal base and declivity meeting almost at a right angle, the former convex in profile, the latter straight; spines long, acute and rather slender, distinctly shorter than the base of the epinotum, directed obliquely upward, backward and outward and continued forward as a pair of blunt, subparallel ridges on the base of the epinotum. All the thoracic spines, except the inferior pronotal pair, covered with small tubercles. Petiole from above oblong, slightly longer than broad, abruptly narrowed anteriorly into a short peduncle; node with four equidistant acute teeth. Postpetiole trapezoidal, more than twice as broad as the petiole, as long as the petiole, as long as broad, semicircularly impressed in the middle behind but with straight, entire posterior border. The border of the impressed region and the sides beset with small tubercles. Gaster suboblong, slightly broadest behind the middle, narrowed in front; first segment with prominent lateral ridges and three broad longitudinal depressions on the dorsal surface. Tubercles small and acute, absent in the median depression and on the ventral surface. Legs long and like the antennal scapes covered with small tubercles.

Mandibles with shining, coarsely punctate blades, more opaque and finely striated at the base. Remainder of body and appendages opaque, granular.

Hairs brownish, very short and curved, longer on the anterior and inferior portions of the head and legs than on the body. Pubescence whitish, very fine and dilute, confined to the antennal funiculi.

Black; mandibles, except the teeth, thorax, petiole, and postpetiole ferruginous or yellowish; pleuræ more or less clouded with black or fuscous; antennæ, legs and apex of gaster dark brown, middle portions of femora and tibiæ often blackish.

Female. Length: 4.5–5 mm.

Head similar to that of the worker. Pronotum with rather blunt inferior and long and pointed superior spines, which are directed outward and forward and slightly upward. Scutellum convex, its posterior edge excised in the middle and with a pair of acute, laterally compressed teeth. Epinotum with short convex base and longer flattened declivity; spines long, slender and acute, directed backward and somewhat outward. Petiole, postpetiole and gaster like those of the worker, but the first broadest in the middle and constricted behind and the second without tubercles on its upper surface. Wings 6 mm. long.

Surface of body coarsely granular; front and vertex rugulose; mesonotum with longitudinal rows of small tubercles.

Pilosity like that of the worker, but longer on the thorax and gaster.

Head and gaster very dark brown; thorax, pedicel, mandibles, antennæ and legs paler, ferruginous. Pleuræ, two triangular spots on the anterior border of the mesonotum, an oblong blotch on the middle of the same region behind, the paraptera and anterior corners of the scutellum, black or dark brown. Wings smoky brown with darker veins and yellowish costal cell.

Male. Length: 3.5–4.2 mm.

Head small, without the eyes and mandibles nearly as broad as long, with rounded and constricted posterior and very prominent ocellar region. Eyes large and convex, their posterior orbits at the middle of the head. Mandibles acute, denticulate, but rather feeble. Clypeus with straight, entire anterior border. Antennæ very slender; scapes surpassing the posterior corners of the head by about ½ their length. Pronotum with very small, acute superior spines and the inferior spines reduced to angles on the lower border of the segment. Mesonotum and scutellum convex, the former with distinct but shallow Mayrian furrows, the latter with a pair of small acute teeth on the posterior border. Epinotum with short, convex base and longer sloping and concave declivity; spines short, acute, not longer than the base and hardly longer than broad at their insertions. Petiole and postpetiole like those of the worker, but the former narrowed behind the middle and the latter with more obscure tubercles. Gaster elliptical, broadest in the middle tapering behind, without depressions and ridges on the first segment and with very minute piligerous tubercles on both the dorsal and ventral surfaces. Genitalia small and retracted. Legs very slender, without tubercles; terminal tarsal joint slightly enlarged. Wings large, 5.5 mm. long.

Whole body and appendages opaque, minutely granular; head finely and longitudinally rugulose behind. Mesonotum with longitudinal rows of shallow oblong depressions or foveolæ. Mesopleuræ feebly rugulose.

Hairs like those of the worker and female, but finer, straighter and more appressed on the legs and antennæ.

Dull, rather light ferruginous; posterior portion of head, Mayrian furrows, lateral borders and a large oblong spot on the posteromedian portion of the mesonotum, paraptera and sides of the scutellum black. Wings like those of the female.

West Indies: Jamaica (T. D. A. Cockerell); St. Vincent (H. Smith); Andros and New Providence Is., Bahamas (Wheeler); Culebra (Wheeler).

I believe there can be no doubt that Forel's *T. sharpi*, André's *jamaicensis* and my *maritima* are all the same species.   I have recently found in the collection of the Philadelphia Academy of Sciences a few workers from Jamaica, which agree very closely with André's description and with my specimens of *maritima* from the Bahamas. These, in turn, are almost identical with specimens collected from a greater number of colonies in the island of Culebra. Prof. Forel, to whom specimens from the latter locality were sent, pronounces them to be "indistinguishable from small specimens of *sharpi*." André's name *jamaicensis* must stand, however, as his description was published some six months earlier than Forel's. So far as known, therefore, there is only a single widely distributed species of *Trachymyrmex* in the West Indies, although there is an allied form (*T. urichi* Forel) in Trinidad and a subspecies of this (*fuscatus* Emery) and several distinct species of the subgenus on the adjacent South American continent.

T. jamaicensis is readily distinguished from all of our North American species by the peculiar coloration of the worker and female, the structure of the frontal and postorbital carinæ, the shape of the petiole and postpetiole, etc.   The male is peculiar in coloration, the shape of the head, and in having very small, concealed genitalia.

9. Atta (Mycetosoritis) hartmanni subgen. et sp. nov.

Worker. (Pl. XLIX, Figs. 6 and 7.) Length: 1.8–2 mm.

Head, without the mandibles, longer than broad, but little broader behind than in front, with broadly and obtusely excised posterior margin, subparallel sides and rather acute posterior corners. Eyes moderately convex, just in front of the middle of the head. Mandibles convex, with two large, acute apical and several small and indistinct basal teeth. Clypeus moderately convex, with entire, broadly rounded anterior margin. Frontal area large, triangular, distinct. Frontal carinæ with very large, broad, flattened lobes anteriorly overlapping the insertions of the antennæ. These lobes have acute anterolateral corners and are separated by distinct reëntrant angles from the posterior ridges which are straight, diverging and continued back to the posterior corners of the head. Lateral carinæ continued back only a little behind the eyes where they turn in but fail to meet the frontal carinæ, though leaving a marked groove for the accommodation of the scape and extending to the posterior corner. Antennæ robust, scapes somewhat thickened distally, reaching with their tips to the posterior corners. Thorax long and stout, especially in front, though decidedly narrower than the head. Pronotum without inferior spines, with a pair of obtuse spines at the humeral angles and a pair of tubercles in the middle almost as far apart as each is from a lateral spine. Mesonotum with a blunt ridge on each side, somewhat higher in front and behind than in the middle. These ridges converge rapidly behind and just in front of the deep mesoëpinotal constriction. Epinotum in profile with subequal base and declivity, the former convex, especially in front, with a pair of ridges diverging posteriorly and continued into the small rather blunt spines, which are but little longer than broad at their bases, and directed upward, backward and outward. Epinotal declivity sloping, concave. Petiole from above suboblong, broader than long, a little broader behind than in front where it is suddenly constricted into a short peduncle; node above with a pair of rather acute teeth. Postpetiole 1½ times as broad as the petiole, broader behind than in front, sides slightly rounded, posterior border angularly excised in the middle. Gaster suboblong, broader behind than in front, not impressed in the middle above, anterior and lateral borders straight, the latter with indistinct longitudinal ridges. Legs rather long and stout.

Opaque throughout; mandibles very finely striated, especially at the base. Body very finely granular; front and vertex longitudinally rugulose; first gastric segment covered uniformly with minute tubercles.

Hairs whitish, suberect, curved and short on the body and appendages, longer and more conspicuous on the clypeus and mandibles.

Ferruginous brown; upper surface of head more or less blackish.

Female. Length: 2.5–2.7 mm.

Head resembling that of the worker, anterolateral corners of frontal carinæ more acute; ocelli very small and indistinct. Pronotum large, with a pair of stout, acuminate superior spines directed forward, outward and upward. Mesonotum small, elliptical, flattened, somewhat narrowed in front, with distinct but shallow Mayrian furrows. Scutellum as long as broad, with excised posterior border and acute posterior angles. Epinotum with short, convex base, long concave and vertical declivity and short spines directed backward and outward. Petiole, postpetiole and gaster resembling those of the worker. Wings short (2 mm.) and rounded; venation like that of *Trachymyrmex* and *Cyphomyrmex* but with the inner branch of the cubital and the distal segment of the externomedian veins very faint or obsolete.

Like the worker in sculpture, pilosity and coloration, but with the mesonotum longitudinally rugulose. Scutellum and paraptera darker than the remainder of the thorax. Wings opaque, fuscous; yellowish towards the base and costal margin.

Male. (Pl. XLIX, Fig. 8.) Length: 2 mm.

Head, without the eyes and mandibles, but little longer than broad, broader behind than in front, with flattened occipital region and a longitudinal ridge on each side of the rather acute posterior corners. Eyes large and convex, the posterior orbits a little behind the middle of the head. Mandibles like those of the worker in shape but smaller and feebler. Clypeus with entire, rounded anterior margin. Lobes of frontal carinæ similar to those of the worker but erect; their posterior ridges short and meeting the lateral carinæ. Scapes very short, extending only a little distance beyond the posterior corners of the head; funicular joints cylindrical, joints 1–7 less than twice as long as broad, terminal joints somewhat longer. Pronotum with short, acute superior spines; inferior spines absent. Mesonotum with distinct Mayrian furrows. Paraptera produced posteriorly as short teeth. Scutellum like that of the female. Epinotum with subequal base and declivity, the former convex, the latter concave; spines about half as long as the base, blunt, somewhat curved, directed upward and outward. Petiole and postpetiole like those of the worker, but the former proportionally longer, the latter broader. Gaster elliptical, median genital appendages digitiform, with blunt tips. Hypopygium with entire rounded posterior margin. Legs rather stout; terminal tarsal joints not enlarged.

Opaque; mandibles and gaster faintly shining; the former very finely, the body more coarsely and densely punctate. Head, thorax and postpetiole also irregularly reticulate-rugulose; first gastric segment above with minute, acute and uniformly distributed tubercles.

Hairs like those of the worker; more distinct and scattered on the gaster.

Head, thorax and pedicel black; first gastric segment very dark brown; remaining gastric segments, mandibles, antennæ and legs light brown or yellowish, antennal scapes, coxæ, and middle portions of the femora infuscated. Wings like those of the female.

Texas: Montopolis and Delvalle, near Austin (Wheeler).

This species which I take pleasure in dedicating to my former pupil, Mr. C. G. Hartmann, who aided me in excavating the nests of this and other Texan Attii, may be regarded either as a degenerate and simplified *Trachymyrmex* or as an aberrant *Cyphomyrmex*. It resembles the species of *Trachymyrmex* in its form and pilosity, while it approaches the species of *Cyphomyrmex* in its small size, the very large lobes of the frontal carinæ, the reduction of the cephalic and thoracic spines and the absence of tubercles on the greater portion of the body. In 1887 (Verh. zool. bot. Ges. Wien, XXXVII pp. 561, 562) Mayr described an aberrant female Attiine ant from Brazil as *Cyphomyrmex asper*, which, though considerably larger than the above described species, would seem nevertheless to belong to the same subgenus. More recently Emery (Bull. Soc. Ent. Ital., XXXVI, 1905, pp. 162, 163) has described and figured a single worker specimen from Chubut, Argentina, as dubiously referable to Mayr's species. This specimen meas-

ures 3 mm. in length and has no reëntrant notch between the anterior lobular
and posterior ridge-like portions of the frontal carinæ, and the shape of the
thorax appears to differ considerably from that of *hartmanni*. Emery, to
whom I sent some workers of this latter form, says, however, that both
species "connetano tra loro i generi *Atta* e *Cyphomyrmex*; é dubbio a quale
dei due convenga meglio assegnarli." As I shall show in the latter part of
this paper, the habits of *hartmanni* are much more like those of *Trachymyrmex* than *Cyphomyrmex*, so that the subgenus *Mycetosoritis*, which I have
erected for this species and *aspera* Mayr, belongs rather with *Atta* s. lat. *M.*
hartmanni should be regarded as the type of this subgenus as Mayr's species
is so imperfectly known.

10. **Atta** (**Mycocepurus**) **smithi** *Forel.*

Atta (Mycocepurus) smithii FOREL, Trans. Ent. Soc. London. 1893, p. 370.   ♀.

Worker. (Pl. XLIX, Figs. 15 and 16.) Length: 2.2–2.5 mm.

Head, without the mandibles, slightly longer than broad, a little broader in
front than behind, with obtusely excised posterior border, pointed posterior corners
and rather convex sides. There is a distinct though shallow occipital groove. Eyes
moderately convex, just behind the middle of the head. Mandibles narrow, acute,
with oblique, 5-toothed blades. Clypeus short and broad, with entire, nearly
straight anterior border. Frontal carinæ with small rounded lobes, very close together and separated only by a narrow, cuneate groove; they are continued behind
as low diverging ridges which fade away before reaching the posterior corners.
Postorbital carinæ indistinct, reaching the posterior corners but not including with
the frontal ridges distinct grooves for the accommodation of the antennal scapes.
Scapes much shorter than the funiculi, slightly thickened towards their tips, which
barely surpass the posterior corners of the head. Thorax long, in front about $\frac{2}{3}$ as
broad as the head, with deep mesoëpinotal constriction. Pronotum without inferior
spines, above with four upwardly directed spines arranged in an arc with its convexity
directed forward; the two outer spines longest and each with a small acute tooth in
front of its base; the inner pair of spines small. Mesonotum also with an arc of four
spines but with its convexity directed backward, so that the spines on both segments
form a broad ellipse. The anterior mesothoracic spines are longer than the posterior
pair. There is also a pair of small projections close together near the anterior borders
of the mesonotum and in the middle of the ellipse. Epinotum with the base fully
twice as long as the declivity, the former with four successive pairs of spines, the
first and third very short and acute, the second longer and the fourth, representing
the typical epinotal spines of other Attii, fully as long as the declivity, slender,
pointed, directed upward and slightly backward and outward, curved inward at
their tips. Metasternum with a small blunt tooth on each side. Petiole from above
narrow, fully twice as long as broad, somewhat violin-shaped, broader behind than
in front, constricted just in front of the node which is cuboidal, with a concave surface and each of the four upper corners produced into a small spine. In profile its
upper surface is horizontal, its anterior slope long and concave. Postpetiole nearly
four times as broad as the petiole and nearly as broad as long, campanulate, with

four longitudinal ridges of which the median pair are blunter and separated by a longitudinal groove deepening suddenly at the posterior margin of the segment to form a somewhat circular pit. Gaster much smaller than the head, fully ⅓ longer than broad, widest posteriorly, with straight sides and anterior border and acute anterior angles. The first segment has a sharp longitudinal ridge on each side but no median depression. Legs long and rather stout.

Opaque throughout; mandibles very finely striated; head above irregularly reticulate-rugose, more coarsely behind than in front. Remainder of body and appendages very finely and obscurely punctate-granular and faintly reticulate, except the gaster which is more distinctly and evenly punctate and slightly roughened on its upper surface. Legs and scapes also slightly scabrous.

Hairs yellowish; very short, curved and sparse, subreclinate, most distinct on the ga ter and appendages. Pubescence very fine, whitish, confined to the antennal funiculi.

Yellowish ferruginous; upper surface of head and gaster and the ridges and tips of the spines darker. Mandibular teeth black.

St. Vincent: Bellisle (H. H. Smith).

Cuba.

I have redescribed this species from a type specimen kindly sent me by Professor Forel who has also described a closely related species, *M. gœldii*, from Brazil. The subgenus *Mycocepurus*, as Forel has shown, is related to the other subgenera of *Atta* on the one hand and to *Cyphomyrmex* and *Myrmicocrypta* on the other. It is peculiar and aberrant, however, in its small size, its small, closely approximated frontal lobes and spinulation. Hitherto *M. smithi* has been known only from St. Vincent. I have received specimens from Cuba. Among the materials in my collection I find also a number of workers from two other localities and representing the following varieties:

11. Atta (**Mycocepurus**) smithi var. borinquenensis var. nov.

Porto Rico: Vega Baja, Arecibo, Utuado, Monte Mandios (Wheeler).

The workers of this form resemble the type very closely in size, coloration and sculpture but have on each side of the occipital furrow at the postero-median border of the head, a distinct tooth which is nearly as large as the teeth which form the posterior corners. The posterior epinotal spines are curved inward at their tips as in the type.

12. Atta (**Mycocepurus**) smithi var. tolteca var. nov.

Mexico: Tuxpan, Jalisco (J. F. McClendon).

Closely resembling the type, but of a yellow color and with straight, more acute and more erect posterior epinotal spines and feebler cephalic sculpture.   The two median occipital teeth of *borinquenensis* are represented by low, pointed ridges.

13. Cyphomyrmex rimosus *Spinola.*

Cryptocerus ? rimosus SPINOLA, Mem. Accad. Sci. Torino (2), XIII, 1851, p. 65 no. 49, ☿ ♂.
Cryptocerus rimosus F. SMITH, Trans. Ent. Soc. London (2), II, 7, 1854, p. 223, no. 28.
Meranoplus difformis F. SMITH, Catalog. Hymen. Brit. Mus., VI, 1858, p. 195, no. 7, ☿.
Cryptocerus rimosus F. SMITH, Trans. Ent. Soc. London (3), I, 4, 1862, p. 409, no. 11, ☿.
Meranoplus difformis F. SMITH, Trans. Ent. Soc. London (3), I, 4, 1862, p. 413, no. 7, ☿.
Cyphomyrmex deformis MAYR, Verh. zool. bot. Ges. Wien, XXXVII, 1887, p. 558, ☿ ♀ ♂ (in part).
Cyphomyrmex rimosus DALLA TORRE, Catalog. Hymen., VII, 1893, p. 150 (in part).
Cyphomyrmex rimosus EMERY, Bull. Soc. Ent. Ital., XXVI, 1894, pp. 88, 89.
Cyphomyrmex rimosus URICH, Trinidad Field Nat. Club, II, no. 7, 1895, p. 181.
Cyphomyrmex rimosus FOREL, Biol. Centr.-Am., Hymen., III, 1899–1900, p. 40.

The typical form of this widely distributed and variable species appears to be confined to northern South America and the adjacent mainland of Central America and Mexico.   It is represented in my collection by a few worker and female specimens from Grenada, Nicaragua (C. T. Baker) and a number of workers from Manatee, British Honduras (J. D. Johnson). In these specimens the postpetiole of the worker is less than twice as broad as long and the color is of a rich yellowish brown, with the head and posterior portion of the gaster clouded with dark brown.   In the female the post-petiole is scarcely broader in proportion to its length and has a perfectly straight posterior border.   According to Emery the male has a relatively narrow head, with very acute posterior angles and the postpetiole is less than 1½ times as broad as long.   A single worker in my possession from Hayti (P. J. Schmitt) approaches the typical *rimosus* more closely than the Central American specimens, as its thoracic protuberances are longer and more acute and the postpetiole is only 1½ times as broad as long.   The following variety, according to Emery (*in litteris*), approaches the typical *rimosus* very closely except in its darker color.

14. Cyphomyrmex rimosus var. comalensis *var. nov.*

Worker.   (Pl. XLIX, Fig. 1.)   Length: 1.8–2 mm.
Head, without the mandibles, longer than broad, much narrower in front than behind, with obtusely excised posterior margin and rather sharply angular posterior

corners. Eyes moderately convex, near the middle of the head. Mandibles small, 5-toothed. Clypeus short on the sides, with a triangular median portion which has a rounded, raised and entire anterior border. Behind it is wedged in between the frontal carinæ which are dilated in front to form two large horizontal lobes impressed in the middle, rounded on the sides, bluntly angular in front and separated at the level of the eye by a reëntrant angle from the posterior ridges. These diverge and extend to the posterior corners of the head where they meet the postorbital ridges and form with them rounded ear-like lobes. Each postorbital ridge is furnished with a blunt but distinct tooth just behind the eye. The frontal and postorbital ridges enclose a deep groove for the accommodation of the antennal scape. Vertex of head with a pair of low, rounded elevations. Antennal scapes robust, thickened towards their tips which extend a little beyond the posterior corners of the head; funiculi slender at the base; joints 2–8 slightly broader than long. Pronotum with four blunt protuberances above in a transverse row, the lateral pair larger and more angular, the inner pair small and closer together than to the lateral pair. Mesonotum a little longer than broad, broader in front than behind, on each side with a blunt ridge, nearly interrupted in the middle so that in certain lights the mesonotum seems to bear two pairs of blunt, elongated elevations. Mesoëpinotal constriction very short and rather deep. Epinotum with a convex base, which is considerably shorter than the sloping, flattened declivity, and with a pair of anteriorly converging ridges. The spines are represented by very small, blunt elevations at the posterior ends of these ridges. Petiole somewhat more than twice as broad as long, flattened above, with rounded sides, only ⅔ as broad as the postpetiole, which is twice as broad as long, convex in front and with a feeble excision in its posterior border. In front of this excision there is a distinct elongate median depression. Gaster suboblong, somewhat longer than broad, with a very short and indistinct median depression at the anterior border. Legs long and stout; hind femora bent and angularly dilated near the base on the flexor side.

Opaque throughout; mandibles very finely and densely striated; remainder of body minutely granular.

Hairs white, short, scale-like, appressed and uniformly distributed, more slender on the legs than on the body. Pubescence very fine, whitish, confined to the mandibles and funiculi.

Very dark brown, upper surface of head and gaster black, anterior portions of the frontal lobes, antennal scapes and tibiæ dark brown; remainder of legs, funiculi and mandibles light brown.

Female. Length: 2.2–2.4 mm.

Head very similar to that of the worker. Pronotum with pointed inferior angles at the coxal insertions, and above with a pair of blunt angular projections which are as broad at their bases as long. Mesonotum anteriorly with a longitudinal median depression and distinct Mayrian furrows, so that its surface is separated into four slightly convex, elongated areas, two anterior and two posterolateral. Epinotum with very short, convex base and long, abrupt and concave declivity; spines blunt, laterally compressed, shorter than broad at their bases. Scutellum flattened, broader than long; its posterior margin excised in the middle and produced as a broad tooth on each side. Pedicel, gaster and legs similar to those of the worker, but the postpetiole nearly three times as broad as long, with nearly straight posterior border.

Like the worker in sculpture and pilosity.

Head, postpetiole, gaster and appendages colored as in the worker. Thorax dark brown, mesonotum and scutellum blackish, each of the convex areas of the former with a reddish brown spot. Wings opaque, smoky brown, with pale veins.

Male. Length: 2.3 mm.

Head, including the eyes, about as broad as long, with straight posterior border and acute posterior angles. Eyes large and convex, in front of the middle of the head. Ocelli projecting. Mandibles rather slender, with two apical and no basal teeth. Clypeus convex, with very faintly notched anterior border. Lobes of frontal carinæ like those of the worker but erect; posterior ridges obsolete. Antennæ slender; scapes suddenly thickened towards their tips and surpassing the posterior corners of the head by nearly ½ their length; funicular joints cylindrical, less than twice as long as broad except the four terminal joints which are longer; first funicular joint thicker than the others. Thorax similar to that of the female but much more slender; basal surface of epinotum longer; spines short and rather acute. Petiole and postpetiole like those of the worker, but the former segment is proportionally longer and the latter has the median depression further forward. Gaster elliptical, slightly flattened; first segment in front with a narrow, faintly impressed line. Genitalia retracted. Legs slender; hind femora without a triangular projection on the flexor side.

Opaque; gaster finely shagreened and distinctly shining.

Appressed white hairs less scale-like and conspicuous than in the worker and female, especially on the gaster; very short on the legs and antennal scapes.

Coloration similar to that of the worker; terminal gastric segments, legs and antennæ dull yellowish brown. Wings as in the female.

Texas: Sources of the Comal River at New Braunfels (Wheeler).

15. Cyphomyrmex rimosus var. fuscus *Emery.*

Emery, Bull. Soc. Ent. Ital., XXVI, 1894, p. 89, ☿ ♀ ♂.

In this variety, described from Santa Catharina, Brazil, all three phases are "entirely brown; mandibles, funiculi and articulations reddish; stature a little more robust" than the typical form.

16. Cyphomyrmex rimosus var. major *Forel.*

Forel, Ann. Soc. Ent. Belg. XLV, 1901, p. 125.   ☿.

In the worker of this variety from Guatemala the stature is somewhat larger (2.7–2.8 mm.) than that of the typical form, the ear-like corners of the head longer and the thoracic ridges and projections more prominent.

17. Cyphomyrmex rimosus minutus *Mayr*.

Cyphomyrmex minutus MAYR, Verh. zool. bot. Ges. Wien, XII, 1862, p. 691 no. 1 ⚥.
Cataulacus deformis ROGER, Berl. entom. Zeitschr., VII, 1863, p. 210, no. 104, ♀ ♂.
Cyphomyrmex steinheili FOREL, Bull. Soc. Vaud. Sc. Nat. (2) XX, 91, 1884, p. 368,
    ⚥,
Cyphomyrmex deformis MAYR, Verh. zool. bot. Ges. Wien, XXXVIII, 1887, p. 558,
    ⚥ ♀ ♂ (in part).
Cyphomyrmex rimosus DALLA TORRE, Catalog. Hymen., VII, 1893, p. 150 (in part).
Cyphomyrmex rimosus FOREL, Trans. Ent. Soc. London, 1893, Pt. IV, p. 374.
Cyphomyrmex rimosus subsp. *minutus* EMERY, Bull. Soc. Ent. Ital., XXVI, 1894,
    p. 89, ⚥ ♂.
Cyphomyrmex rimosus FOREL, Biol. Centr.-Am., Hymen., III, 1899–1900, p. 40
    (in part).
Cyphomyrmex rimosus subsp. *minutus* WHEELER, Bull. Am. Mus. Nat. Hist., XXI,
    1905, p. 106, figs. N. and O.

Venezuela: Cayenne (Emery).

West Indies: Cuba (Mayr); St. Vincent (H. H. Smith); New Providence, Bahamas (Wheeler); Culebra and Porto Rico (Wheeler).

Florida: Planter, Key Largo (Wheeler).

This subspecies which is confined to the West Indies and adjacent shores of North and South America, appears to differ very slightly from the typical form of the species and the var. *comalensis*. The worker is somewhat smaller and often of a paler color, with the thoracic projections more feebly developed and more rounded and the vestiges of the epinotal spines even more insignificant. Both the petiole and postpetiole are considerably broader, each being fully twice as broad as long. According to Emery the male of *minutus* has the head rounded behind, but my specimens from the Bahamas and Porto Rico have the posterior border of the head straight and the posterior angles projecting as acute teeth. In the female the epinotum is very steep, with small, blunt spines. Forel seems never to have accepted this subspecies, and I am myself very doubtful whether it deserves to rank as such. It is certainly much less distinct and less easily recognizable than the following:

18. Cyphomyrmex rimosus dentatus *Forel*.

Cyphomyrmex rimosus race *dentatus* FOREL, Ann. Soc. Ent. Belg., XLV, 1901, p. 124
    ⚥.
Cyphomyrmex rimosus subsp. *dentatus* WHEELER, Ann. Soc. Ent. Belg., XLV, 1901,
    p. 200.

Mexico: Cuernavaca (Wheeler).

The worker of this marked subspecies is described by Forel as follows: "Differs from the type in that the basal surface of the epinotum has two distinct teeth. The pronotal protuberances are stronger, more dentiform. The occipital ears are a little more pronounced than in the type of the species, and especially form a more complete and larger groove for the scape which surpasses them little if at all. Entirely pale ferruginous yellow, with the front and vertex indistinctly brown. The petiole is also broader. The postpetiole has a strong median notch at the middle of its posterior border and its sides are prolonged as dentiform cones which are curved backward. The sculpture is that of *rimosus*, but the gaster has a distinct but very fine system of minute, blunt tubercles. The pubescence is extremely short and very fine, not dilated nor brilliant, so that it is inconspicuous."

Two deälated females of *dentatus* in my collection measure 2.4 mm. in length, and have prominent but blunt and upturned prothoracic spines and strong laterally compressed epinotal teeth; the epinotal declivity is very concave, the posterolateral cones of the postpetiole are more prominent and the median dorsal region of the same segment is more concave than in the worker. The head and thorax are much rougher than in the females of the typical *rimosus* and the gaster is more strongly tubercular, with a short but deep median depression at the base of the first segment. The body is dark brown, the upper surface of the head and thorax blackish and covered with a bluish bloom.

19. Cyphomyrmex rimosus transversus *Emery*.

Cyphomyrmex rimosus subsp. *transversus* EMERY, Bull. Soc. Ent. Ital., XXVI, 1894, p. 90, ☿ ♀ ♂.

Cyphomyrmex dentatus race *olindanus* FOREL, Ann. Soc. Ent. Belg., XLV, 1901, p. 337, ☿.

Cyphomyrmex rimosus transversus EMERY, Bull. Soc. Ent. Ital., XXXVIII, 1905, p. 161, ☿ ♀ ♂.

Brazil: Matto Grosso (Emery); Ceara and Olinda (P. J. Schmitt).

The worker of this subspecies resembles *dentatus* in sculpture and in the development of the thoracic projections, but the appressed hairs on the body are broader and more scale-like even than in the typical *rimosus*, the petiole and postpetiole broader, and the median dorsal impression on the latter and on the base of the first gastric segment deeper and longer. The epinotum has blunt but distinct teeth.

In the female the epinotal teeth are very large, compressed and obtuse, the pedicel even broader than in the worker.

The male has the posterior border of the head broadly excised and the posterior corners with acute, slightly recurved teeth. Except in pilosity *transversus* is closely related to *dentatus*, as Forel has observed.

20.   Cyphomyrmex rimosus salvini *Forel.*

Cyphomyrmex rimosus race *salvini* FOREL, Biol. Centr.-Am., Hymen., III, 1899–1900, p. 40, pl. iii, fig. 2.   ♀.

Forel described only the female of this form from a specimen taken at Bugaba, Panama. The late Dr. F. C. Paulmier brought me from Port Limon, Costa Rica two males and several workers which seem to me to belong to this same form. The worker is larger than that of any of the other subspecies of *rimosus*, measuring nearly 2.5 mm. The frontal lobes are very large and concave, the ear-like corners of the head much prolonged and pointed. The thoracic projections, especially the anterior pronotal pair, are long and acute, the epinotal teeth very faintly indicated. The petiole is more than twice as broad as long, the postpetiole about 1½ times as broad as long, with excised posterior margin and a posteromedian impression. There is also a distinct median impression at the base of the gaster. The hairs are much flattened and scale-like, pearly white and abundant, appressed on the body, but reclinate or even suberect on the legs and scapes. The body is light chocolate brown, the legs and antennæ paler.

The female according to Forel's description, measures 3.7 mm. and is very similar to the worker in the shape of the head. The superior pronotal teeth are stout and triangular, the epinotal teeth much reduced. The postpetiole is proportionally broader than in the worker, the gaster very convex, feebly marginate on the sides and without any indications of depressions and elevations.

The male, too, is decidedly larger than the corresponding sex in other forms of *rimosus*, measuring nearly 3 mm. in length. The superior occipital teeth are short and acute, the superior pronotal pair blunt and rather slender. In the place of the spines, the epinotum has a pair of broad, laterally compressed projections, which are continued forward and backward on the base and declivity as prominent ridges. The hairs on the body and appendages are all appressed and not very abundant, not dilated on the legs and only slightly scale-like on the body. The latter is chocolate brown like that of the worker, with the first gastric segment blackish, the mandibles, clypeus, frontal lobes, antennæ, legs, terminal gastric segments and genitalia dull yellow. The wings are very dark brown or blackish.

21. Cyphomyrmex wheeleri *Forel.*

Forel, Bull. Soc. Ent. Suisse, X, 7, 1900, pp. 282–284, ☿ ♀.

Worker. (Pl. XLIX, Fig. 2.) Length: 2.–2.5 mm.

Head, without the mandibles, longer than broad, broader behind than in front, with obtusely excised posterior margin and rather sharp, ear-like posterior corners. Eyes moderately large, convex, at the middle of the head. Mandibles acute, with five sharp teeth. Clypeus with thin, entire anterior border. Frontal area triangular. Frontal carinæ with large, rounded anterior lobes, each with a circular impression, and continued back as a pair of strong, straight, diverging ridges to the posterior corners, where they loop around and become continuous with the postorbital carinæ. thus enclosing deep grooves for the antennal scapes. Each postorbital carina bears a prominent tooth just behind the eye. Vertex with a pair of short longitudinal ridges as far apart as each is from the posterior ridge of a frontal carina and continued laterally along the occipital border to the posterior corner. Here also the 'ears' are joined by a pair of prominent ridges from the posteroinferior surface of the head. Antennal scapes very slender at the base, enlarged towards the tips which reach the posterior corners of the head; joints 2–8 of the funiculus a little broader than long. Pronotum with a pair of acute inferior teeth and above with a larger pair of angular humeral projections and a median pair of smaller projections. Mesonotum elevated in the middle in the form of an elongate elliptical, slightly concave disc, truncated behind, with a faint transverse depression on its posterior portion and bordered with a prominent ridge which is interrupted in the middle in front. Mesoëpinotal constriction short and deep. Epinotum as high as the mesonotum, its base very convex and nearly as long as the concave declivity with which it forms an obtuse angle in profile. Spines laterally compressed, short and triangular, as broad at the base as long, directed backward and continued forward and backward as ridges on the base and declivity. There is also a pair of lateral ridges on the base. Petiole nearly twice as broad as long, as broad in front as behind, with rounded anterior angles; node short, compressed anteroposteriorly, with two spines, directed upward and backward. Postpetiole trapezoidal, 1½ times as broad as the petiole and less than twice as broad as long, with two blunt anterior, two larger and more rounded posterior protuberances and a broad, longitudinal depression in the middle; posterior border entire. Gaster suboblong, distinctly longer than broad, as broad in front as behind; first segment convex above, with distinct lateral ridges and a faint median depression at the base. Tibiæ somewhat compressed; hind femora curved, angularly dilated and compressed near the base on the flexor side.

Opaque throughout; mandibles very finely and indistinctly striated. Remainder of body very finely granular-punctate; antennal grooves and gaster densely and distinctly punctate.

Hairs short, glistening white, scale-like and appressed, uniformly distributed over the appendages and upper surface of the body. Pubescence very fine, whitish, confined to the antennal funiculi.

Yellowish ferruginous; mandibular teeth black.

Female. Length: 2.5–2.7 mm.

Very similar to the worker. Pronotum with prominent inferior and superior teeth, the former acute, the latter larger and blunt. Mesonotum prominent, flattened, with a faint median furrow anteriorly and a pair of broader Mayrian furrows. Scutellum with very broadly and faintly excised posterior border separating a pair of broad, acute teeth. Epinotum with the base convex and only about half as long as the abrupt concave declivity; spines similar to those of the worker but somewhat stouter.

Sculpture and pilosity as in the worker.

Color a little darker in old specimens. Wings opaque, infuscated; the membranes and veins in the anterobasal portion of both fore and hind wings fulvous.

Male. Length: 2.4–2.6 mm.

Head, without the mandibles and eyes, narrow, longer than broad, with straight posterior border. Mandibles like those of the worker but less distinctly denticulate. Frontal carinæ with large, reflected lobes and strong, diverging posterior ridges reaching to the posterior corners where each terminates in a compressed, projecting tooth. Postorbital carinæ absent. Antennæ slender, scapes enlarged towards their tips which surpass the posterior corners of the head by about ⅓ of their length. Pronotum with indistinct inferior, but prominent and acute superior teeth. Mesonotum with distinct Mayrian furrows. Scutellum like that of the female, but with more deeply excised posterior border. Petiole and postpetiole like those of the worker and female. Gaster elliptical, convex above. Legs long and slender. Hind femora not angularly dilated below.

Opaque; very finely and densely punctate; gaster faintly shining or glossy.

Pilosity very similar to that of the worker and female.

Ferruginous; upper surface of head and the thoracic depressions blackish; basal segment of gaster dark brown above. Mandibles, antennæ, legs and tip of gaster yellowish. Wings like those of the female.

Texas: Austin, Belton, Langtry, Fort Davis (Wheeler).

California: Three Rivers (Culbertson).

The types from which the worker and deälated female were carefully described by Forel, are from Austin. The species is allied to the South American *C. strigatus* Mayr and *C. auritus* Mayr but differs from both in having larger frontal lobes and in lacking prominent ridges on the middle of the first gastric segment. The ear-like posterior corners of the head are much shorter than in *auritus* and the scapes are shorter than in *strigatus*.

22. Cyphomyrmex flavidus *Pergande.*

Cyphomyrmex flavidus Pergande, Proc. Calif. Acad. Sci. (2), V, Dec. 1895, p. 895, ☿.
Cyphomyrmex flavidus Forel, Biol. Centr.–Am., Hymen., III, 1899–1900, p. 41.

Worker. Length: 2.2–2.8 mm.

Head, without the mandibles, longer than broad, broader behind than in front, with obtusely excised posterior border and prominent posterior corners. Eyes convex, at the middle of the head. Mandibles small and acute, with oblique, apparently 5-toothed blades. Clypeus long and rather flat, with a minute median excision in its thin anterior border. Frontal area triangular. Lobes of frontal carinæ very large, horizontal, half as long as the head and extending out laterally a little beyond the borders of the head. Posteriorly each of these lobes has a deep subtriangular depression in its surface. The ridges of the frontal carinæ diverge backward to the posterior corners where they pass over into the postorbital carinæ, not through a rounded arc but rectangularly, so that the termination of the antennal groove is broad and truncated. There is a ridge on each side of the inferior occipital portion of the head and a pair of projections on the vertex, which are continued laterally along the occipital border as a pair of blunt ridges to the posterior corners. Antennal scapes enlarged towards the tips, which extend a little beyond the posterior corners; joints 2–7 of the funiculus a little broader than long. Thorax robust; pronotum with a pair of acute inferior teeth, which are directed forward, and a blunt protuberance on each side above. Mesonotum in the form of an elevated, elliptical and slightly concave disc, bordered with a low ridge which is interrupted in the middle behind and in the middle on each side. This ridge bears a pair of rounded swellings just in front of its lateral interruptions. Mesoëpinotal constriction deep and narrow. Epinotum with a pair of swellings at its base; declivity sloping, longer than the base; spines reduced to a pair of laterally compressed and rather acute teeth which are as long as they are broad at the base. Petiole and postpetiole resembling each other in shape, the former twice as broad as long, broader behind where its sides are produced as a pair of blunt angles; it is flattened above, without spines or teeth and with a small semicircular impression in the middle of its posterior border. Postpetiole ⅓ broader than the petiole, more than twice as broad as long, rounded in front, with a median groove, broadening behind; posterior margin with three semicircular impressions of which the median is the largest. Gaster longer than broad, suboblong, with straight, feebly marginate sides, rounded anterior and posterior borders, and a short median groove at the base of the first segment. Hind femora curved, with an angular, compressed projection near the base on the flexor side.

Opaque throughout, very finely and densely punctate-granular.

Hairs minute, appressed, slightly dilated, glistening white, rather sparse and indistinct. Pubescence fine, whitish, confined to the antennal funiculi.

Ferruginous yellow; clypeus, frontal lobes, front and middle of vertex more or less brownish; mandibular teeth black.

Mexico: Santiago Ixtquintla, Tepic (Eisen and Vaslit).

This species, which I have redescribed from a type specimen kindly sent me by Mr. Pergande, at first sight closely resembles *C. wheeleri*. It may be distinguished, however, by the absence of teeth on the petiole, the much broader and more truncated ear-like corners of the head, longer antennal scapes and much blunter ridges and projections on the thorax. *C. flavidus* is thus intermediate in several respects between *wheeleri* and *rimosus*, but is undoubtedly a distinct species. Although at present known only from northern Mexico, it may be expected to occur as far north as the southern portions of Arizona and California.

23. **Myrmicocrypta brittoni** sp. nov.

Worker. (Pl. L, Figs. 18 and 19.)   Length: 2.3–2.5 mm.

Head, without the mandibles, about as broad as long, slightly broader behind than in front, with obtusely excised posterior border, rather straight sides, rounded posterior corners and a narrow median longitudinal groove. Eyes distinctly in front of the middle, of moderate size and convexity. Mandibles large, convex, with straight outer and inner borders, the latter with about ten teeth which grow gradually smaller towards the base. Clypeus short, with entire, flattened and very broadly rounded anterior border. Frontal carinæ with flattened but slightly reflected lobes, which are much longer than broad, with roundly angular external edges reaching only half the distance between the median line and the external border of the head. Mesially these lobes are fused with the posterior portion of the clypeus and enclose the small, indistinct frontal area which is triangular and longer than broad. The lobes of the frontal carinæ are not continued behind in the form of diverging ridges as in other Attii. Lateral carinæ sharp and distinct, continued to the posterior orbits and bounding a broad, short and deep antennal groove. There are no postorbital carinæ. Antennæ rather slender; scapes slightly curved at the base and enlarged towards their tips, which slightly surpass the posterior corners of the head; funicular joints all considerably longer than broad, terminal joint nearly as long as the four preceding joints together. Thorax long and rather narrow, in front about ⅔ as broad as the head. Pronotum with small, acute inferior angles. There is a pair of blunt epinotal teeth, but otherwise the thorax is smooth and without spines or projections. Mesoëpinotal constriction distinct, but long and rather shallow. Humeral angles rounded, mesonotum about as long as the pronotum, elongate elliptical, flattened, slightly higher than the epinotum. Epinotum with subequal base and declivity, the former straight and horizontal, the latter concave and sloping, without longitudinal ridges. Metasternum with a small rounded tubercle on each side. Petiole oblong, a little broader than long, with slightly rounded anterior and acute posterior corners; node evenly convex above, suddenly constricted anteriorly into a very short peduncle. Postpetiole nearly twice as broad as the petiole, somewhat broader than long, with straight posterior border, rounded anterior corners and straight, subparallel sides; convex and evenly rounded above without a posteromedian impression. Gaster smaller than the head, longer than broad, elliptical, with straight anterior border and convex upper surface, without lateral ridges or median impression on the first segment. Legs slender, hind femora straight and without an angular projection on the flexor side.

Opaque throughout; mandibles slightly glossy, very finely and densely striated; remainder of body very densely and uniformly punctate.

Hairs short, glistening white, dilated and scale-like, appressed, uniformly distributed over the body and appendages. Antennal funiculi and tarsi with delicate whitish pubescence.

Black; clypeus, antennal grooves, inferior corners of pronotum, antennal scapes, coxæ and legs, dark brown; mandibles, except the teeth, tips of scapes, funiculi, tarsi and articulations of legs light brown or yellowish.

Porto Rico: Santurce (Wheeler).

Though at once recognizable as an Attiine ant, this species is nevertheless so unlike any of the species of which I had seen specimens or descriptions that I at first decided to make it the type of a new genus or subgenus. Professor Forel, to whom I sent specimens, has kindly given me a worker of a species which he took some years ago in Colombia. This species, which he will describe as *M. emeryi*, is intermediate in certain characters, such as the structure of the frontal lobes, between the above described *brittoni* and *M. squamosa* F. Smith (= *uncinata* Mayr). *M. emeryi* differs from *brittoni* in having a much longer and more slender thorax, pedicel, legs and antennæ, in being of a lighter (brown) color and in having the appressed hairs on the body and legs, long and not scale-like. The clypeus, lower surfaces of the mandibles and the gula have conspicuously long and projecting hairs. The petiole is nearly twice as long as broad, the postpetiole slightly longer than broad and with a deep rounded excision in the middle of its posterior border. The mandibles are more slender, with more oblique blades and fewer teeth. The epinotal teeth are distinctly longer and directed upward. The frontal carinæ are smaller and the tips of the antennal scapes extend further beyond the posterior corners of the head. According to Mayr's description the thorax in the worker of *squamosa* is furnished with teeth and projections like the more typical Attii. The Porto Rican and Colombian forms therefore approach *Apterostigma* and *Sericomyrmex* much more closely than do the other known species of *Myrmicocrypta* and may be regarded as the simplest and most generalized members of the genus, if not of the whole Attiine tribe. I take great pleasure in dedicating the Porto Rican species to the distinguished botanist, Professor N. L. Britton, with whom I passed many delightful and profitable hours collecting plants and insects in Culebra and Porto Rico.

Part III. Ethological Observations.

1. Atta texana Buckley.

In the United States this large "cutting" or "parasol" ant (Fig. 7, and Pl. XLIX, Figs. 11–14), is the only species of the tribe Attii that forms sufficiently populous colonies to be of any economic importance, or, indeed, to be sufficiently common and conspicuous to attract the attention of any one but a myrmecologist. Although unable to determine its exact range, I have found no indications of its occurrence outside of a rather restricted area in Texas. This area appears to have its center at Austin and to comprise the territory for some hundreds of miles north and south in a narrow belt where there is a moderate annual rain-fall and where the forests are of a mesophytic character.   I have never seen it in the dry western portions of the state nor have I heard of its occurrence in the more humid eastern counties, in Louisiana or the other Gulf States.   It was seen as far south as Alice in Nueces County, and probably occurs as far north as Waco and Fort Worth.   It certainly could not endure the winters of the "Panhandle" region nor even those of the extreme northeastern portion of Texas.   Even in the vicinity of Austin large colonies of *Atta texana* are rather sporadic. It prefers the neighborhood of rivers and creeks and especially the rich soil of the pecan and the pure sand or somewhat clayey soil of the post-oak

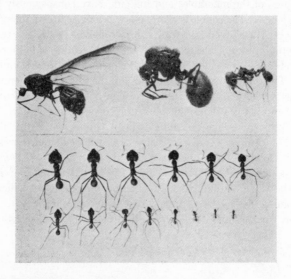

Fig. 7.   *Atta texana* Buckley; male, deälated female, soldier and series of workers; natural size.   (Photograph by Messrs. C. T. Brues and A. L. Melander.)

woods.   In such spots one is always sure of finding it along the banks of the Colorado, Comal and Guadeloupe Rivers.

The nests are nearly always situated in places fully exposed to the sun, in clearings of the woods, in fields, along roads, etc.   In some localities, as at Elgin, I have found them in the sand-ballast of the railway tracks. The nests can be recognized even at a distance as very flat mounds usually not more than one to two dcm. high, with very uneven surface and consisting of sand or soil of a lighter color than the surface of the surrounding country.   Closer inspection shows that these mounds, which may cover an area of many square meters, have been derived from the walls of craters, washed down and fused with one another by the rains. Several perfect and recently constructed craters are commonly found on the top or about the edges of the mound, and in the case of large and active colonies these may be numerous, as in the nest shown in Fig. 8, which was situated on the left bank of the Colorado River between Austin and Montopolis. The craters in this instance covered an area of more than 100 sq. m. although the nest had not been in existence long enough to form a distinct mound. They varied from a dcm. to half a m. in diameter and from a few cm. to a dcm.

Fig. 8. Large *Atta texana* nest on the left bank of the Colorado River between Austin and Montopolis, Texas. (Photograph by Mr. C. G. Hartmann.)

high. Their typical form is shown in Fig. 9, which is taken from the nest represented in the preceding figure. The wall of the crater is often higher on one side than on the others, or it may be crescentic, that is, interrupted at one part of the circumference. The opening at the bottom varies from 3–6 cm. in diameter, is often very irregular in outline and leads vertically or somewhat obliquely downward into a gallery of the same diameter. The large size of the opening is evidently an adaptation for two very different purposes, first, for enabling the ants to carry in their pieces of leaves more easily, and second, for ventilating the subterranean portions of the nest. In the nests of *Atta texana* I have been unable to detect two kinds of craters, one used as entrances, the other for ejecting the exhausted portions of the fungus gardens, as Forel has observed in the Colombian *Atta cephalotes* and as I have observed at Cuernavaca, Mexico, in the nests of *A. mexicana*. All the craters when fresh, consist of large, uniform pellets of earth or sand, 3–5 mm. in diameter, which are carefully compacted and carried to the surface by the workers. The grains of sand or earth seem to be held together merely by the moisture that permeates the soil at the depth from which they are dug, rather than by any salivary secretion such as von Ihering supposes

Fig. 9.   One of the craters of the *Atta texana* nest represented in the preceding figure, about ⅓ natural size.   (Photograph by Mr. C. G. Hartmann.)

the Brazilian *A. sexdens* to employ for this purpose. The pellets disintegrate in the first rain, so that the walls of the craters become lower and more rounded and fuse with one another to form the low mound of older nests. The ants usually work at only a few of the craters at a time, and as only one or two of the openings are used when the ants are busily engaged carrying in leaves, it seems probable that the greater number of craters is constructed for the aëration of the nest and not for entrance or exit.

The depth and extent of the excavations vary, of course, with the size of the colony, its age, and the character of the soil. This is evident from the following notes on three nests examined at different seasons of the year.

April 10, 1900, Messrs. A. L. Melander and C. T. Brues assisted me in excavating a moderately large nest situated at the base of a juniper on the banks of Waller Creek, at Austin.   There were at least twenty craters on the summit of the flat mound, which was about 5 m. across.   These entrances measuring 2.5–4 cm. in diameter, were found to lead downward as tubular galleries converging towards and uniting with one another more and more, till a depth of about a meter was reached.   Here each of the galleries, now greatly reduced in number, entered the top of a large chamber with vaulted roof and level floor.   Some of these chambers were fully 30 cm. in diameter and 25 cm. high and as broad as long, others were much elongated.   They were sometimes connected with one another by means of broad galleries, especially when lying at different levels.   The rootlets of the juniper ran through some of the chambers or hung down freely into their cavities.   Each chamber had a large placenta-like gray or white fungus garden covering the greater portion of its floor.   Small gardens of a more nodular form also hung suspended, enveloping the juniper roots, which seemed to have been left untouched by the ants, during their excavations, for this very purpose. Each garden was a comb-like or sponge-like mass of triturated leaves and juniper berries, permeated and covered with a mould-like mycelium.   This mass exhaled a rather pleasant odor not unlike that of stale honey, and crumbled so readily under the touch that it was impossible to remove it entire.   It swarmed with workers, the soldiers being least, the mimims most numerous, whereas the mediæ were intermediate in numbers as well as in size.   In one of the gardens we found the aged mother queen of the colony, three winged males, and a number of larvæ.   Several of the disintegrated gardens together with many of the ants were carried to the laboratory and placed in large glass jars.   By the following morning the insects had completely rebuilt their gardens.   The coarser work of carrying and building up the particles of leaf-pulp fell to the lot of the mediæ, while the minims went about planting and pruning the tufts of fungus hyphæ.   The huge soldiers merely stalked about on the surface of the gardens, often breaking down under their weight the walls of the delicate comb.   The ants were confined in the jars for several days, and after the expiration of a week I made an observation that did not impress me as important at the time: the gardens, which were in a much less flourishing condition than when first installed in the jars, were seen to be covered with droplets of a brown liquid. As these droplets closely resembled those since described by J. Huber (*vide ante*, p. 698) as the excrement of the female *Atta sexdens*, it is probable that the soldiers and mediæ, unable to add fresh leaves to their rapidly deteriorating gardens, resorted to the very same method of manuring the mycelium as that employed by the queen *Atta* while she is founding her colony.

November 3, 1900, I excavated a large nest of *Atta texana* situated on the left bank of the Colorado River about a mile west of Austin. This nest was in pure sand at the edge of a sorghum field about 15 m. above the river bottom where it was overgrown with low willow, pecan and Texas persimmon trees. The ants were busy defoliating the willows and carrying their leafy burdens up the bank and into the nest along a path about 80 m. long. At intervals along this path piles of leaf-clippings, dropped by the ants, lay drying in the sun. The leaves were cut by the mediæ in the manner described by Mœller for the South American *Acromyrmex discigera*. The

Fig. 10.   Barton Springs, near Austin, Texas, the classic locality for the study of *Atta texana*.   (Photograph by Messrs. Brues and Melander.)

nest was in a promontory accessible from three sides, one of which formed the wall of a small ravine. The craters were very numerous and nearly all on the summit of the bank. The arrangement of the galleries and chambers was very similar to that described for the nest on Waller Creek, except that the chambers were at a lower level (1.5 to 2.3 m.) below the surface and much larger. One of them, of a crescentic form, measured nearly 1 m. in length and 30 cm. broad and high. All of the chambers, of which I examined fully a dozen, were situated in a damper layer of sand than that overlying them and contained huge fungus-gardens on their flattened floors. These gardens were 10–15 cm. high, of a yellowish color below and made up very largely of triturated sorghum leaves. Above they were bluish or greenish gray and this was the only portion that was permeated and covered with the living mycelium, the lower portions having lost their fungus-nourishing substances. The large amount of this exhausted leaf-pulp still retained in the chambers, showed that *Atta texana* must differ from some of the tropical species of this genus, which carry it to the surface

Fig. 11.   Large *Atta texana* nest on the right bank of Barton Creek near Austin, Texas. (Photograph by Messrs. Brues and Melander.)

and eject it from the craters. The Texan species simply keeps on building up its gardens till they reach a considerable thickness while the mycelium retreats to the more nutritive superficial layer. Many of the gardens in the nest under discussion contained worker larvæ and pupæ in abundance, but no sexual forms, either mature or immature. Both in this and in the previously described nest I found many specimens of a little myrmecophilous cockroach, of which I shall have more to say in the sequel. Although the nest was easily excavated, owing to its location in an exposed bank of pure sand, nevertheless I was made very uncomfortable by the attacks of the soldiers, who actually drew blood with their sharp mandibles.

An interesting nest was excavated and measured by Messrs, Brues and Melander during the spring of 1903. This was situated on the right bank of Barton Creek (Fig. 10) near Austin, about 15 m. above the bed of the stream. In surface view (Fig. 11) it presented a low, irregular mound, con-

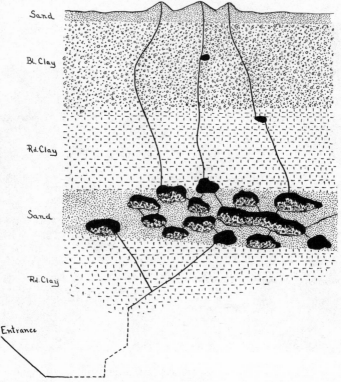

Sand

Bl. Clay

Rd. Clay

Sand

Rd. Clay

Entrance

Fig. 12.   Diagram of the *Atta texana* nest represented in the preceding figure.   (From a sketch by Messrs. Brues and Melander.)

sisting of fused or contiguous craters of pure sand resting on a layer of blue clay. As shown in the diagram, Fig. 12, galleries descended vertically from these craters through the blue clay layer, which was nearly 2 m. thick, and continued down through an equally thick layer of red clay, where they entered a layer of pure sand about a meter in thickness. At the top of this last layer they opened into a number of large chambers communicating with one another by means of short galleries. The chambers occupied the entire layer, so that the total depth of the nest was very nearly 5 m. Some of the chambers broken open by the pick, are represented in Fig. 13. In the lowermost of these one of the large fungus gardens is seen *in situ* resting on the floor. From the lower series of chambers a number of galleries continued down through another layer of clay, and finally united to form a single long gallery, which ran at first horizontally and parallel with the stream, but finally rose obliquely and opened on the surface of the bank

Fig. 13. Exposed chambers of nest represented in the two preceding figures   A large fungus garden is shown *in situ* in the lowermost chamber.   (Photograph by Messrs. Brues and Melander.)

a few meters above the water level and at a distance of fully 65 m. from the nest! This remarkable tunnel was the entrance through which the long file of workers brought the leaf-clippings to the chambers. The crater openings on the top of the bank seemed to be used only for excavating and ventilating purposes. That some of these, however, were the original entrances of the nest was proved by the presence of small dilatations or chambers only a few cm. in diameter in the course of the vertical galleries.

These dilatations, two of which are indicated in the diagram, must have represented the chambers of the incipient nest and one of them was undoubtedly the original cell excavated by the mother queen of the colony.

In collecting the vegetable substances to serve as a substratum on which to grow their fungus, the workers of *Atta texana* seem to show no evidences of discrimination, further than that a colony usually concentrates its attention on one kind of material on each of its forays. I have seen workers of the same colony at different times cutting and carrying home the leaves of plants belonging to the most diverse natural orders. They seem indeed to prefer plants with small or rather narrow leaves, but the texture of the leaves is apparently a matter of little importance, for the ants may be seen defoliating soft herbs like the sheep sorrel (*Rumex acetosella*) or the clover, and anon attacking the tough leathery foliage of the live oak (*Quercus virginiana*). But even hard berries like those of the juniper are collected and embedded entire in the gardens. Once I saw a colony carrying away the cracked grains of maize from a hominy mill, and on another occasion the same colony was assiduously gathering large caterpillar droppings that had rained down from a plane tree near the nest. These ants occasionally enter gardens and defoliate rose-bushes or other ornamental shrubs or destroy tender vegetables, but their inability to concentrate their attacks for several consecutive days on particular species of plants, and the somewhat smaller size of their colonies than those of the tropical *Attæ*, make them much less dangerous economically than might be supposed.

Like many other Texan ants, *Atta texana* is more sensitive to the heat than to the sunlight. I infer this from the fact that during the winter and cool autumn and spring months it forages at all times of the day but during the hot summer months carries on its excavations and goes abroad only during the cool night hours. The sensitiveness of these ants to heat and to the humidity of the air is also shown by the fact that they carefully close their nest craters with earth, leaves, or sticks during hot, dry spells. This seems to be an adaptation for preventing the escape of the moisture from the nest through the large ventilating galleries and the consequent injury to the proliferating mycelia in the gardens. While opening the nest chambers of this and other species of Attii I have often seen the delicate fungi wither up within a few moments after exposure to the dry air.

I have not observed in *Atta texana* the method of comminuting the leaf-clippings but there can be little doubt that it is very much like that employed by *A. cephalotes* and *Acromyrmex discigera* as described by Tanner and Mœller. The macroscopic structure of the gardens (Figs. 14 and 15) has been correctly described by McCook (*ante*, p. 679). Their microscopic structure resembles very closely that of the *Acromyrmex* studied by Mœller.

There is the same beautiful, white mycelium with hyphæ .6–.8 μ in diameter everywhere threading and covering the comb-like leaf-pulp and densely dotted with clusters .2–.3 mm. in diameter of the small spherical or pear-shaped food-bodies (Kohlrabiköpfchen) 3–5.5 μ in diameter. As Mœller's terms for these structures are rather far-fetched, since to English-speaking peoples at least the kohlrabi is by no means a familiar vegetable, and as the structures really deserve somewhat more dignified or at any rate more tech-

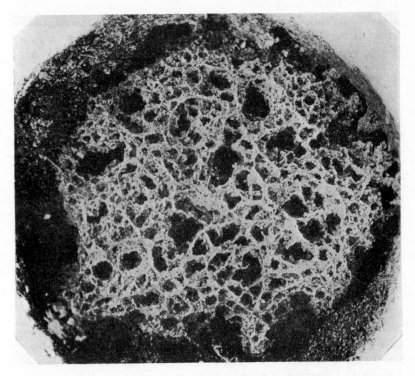

Fig. 14.   Entire fungus garden of *Atta texana*, about ¼ natural size. (Photograph by Messrs. Brues and Melander.)

nical appellations, I would suggest that the globular swellings of the hyphæ be called *gongylidia* and the grape-like clusters which they form, *bromatia*. The arrangement of the leaf-pulp at the surface of the gardens in the form of thin walls or plates greatly extends the exposed surface of the substratum, favors the growth of the plant, and thus increases the amount of it that can be raised in a circumscribed cavity. This arrangement also facilitates the control of the fungus and its cultivation and makes it more accessible as food.

Some well-developed means of intercommunication would seem to be necessary for ants like *Atta texana* which live in great colonies and coöperate so intimately both on their foraging expeditions and in the cultivation of their delicate food plant.   I am convinced that this means is supplied by the stridulatory organs which are highly developed in all the castes of the species. As I have shown in a former paper,[1] the stridulation of the huge females of *Atta texana* is audible when the insect is held a foot or more from the ear. The male and soldier to be audible must be held somewhat closer, the largest workers still closer, whereas the smaller workers and mimins, though stridulating, as may be seen by the rapid movements of the gaster on the postpetiole, are quite inaudible to the human ear.   It is probable that all these

Fig. 15.   Portion of fungus garden of *Atta texana* built up by ants in confinement.   (Photograph by Messrs. Brues and Melander.)

differences in the rate of vibrations, or humanly speaking, of pitch, correlated as it is with a differentiation in the size and functions of the various castes, is a very important factor in the coöperation of these insects, especially in the often widely separated subterranean cavities in which they spend so much of their lives.   Miss Fielde and Prof. Parker[2] have recently given good reasons for concluding that these vibrations are transmitted through the soil or other solids and not through the air, and that they are therefore perceived by the ants through their legs as tactile rather than as

[1] Ethological Observations on an American Ant (Leptothorax Emersoni Wheeler). Arch. f. Psychol. u. Neurol., II, 1903, p. 19, foot-note.
[2] The Reactions of Ants to Material Vibrations.   Proc. Acad. Nat. Sci. Phila., Sept. 1904, pp. 642–650.

auditory sensations. This result agrees also with the accounts of others who have investigated the perception of vibrations in insects.

Of all ants the Attii would seem, at first thought, to offer in the great sponge-like masses of decomposing vegetable matter of their fungus gardens the most favorable of resorts for all kinds of myrmecophiles and synœketes. But the number of such animals hitherto observed in the nests of these ants is very small. This is probably due to the exquisite care and diligence with which the ants patrol and cultivate all parts of their gardens to prevent the growth of the aërial hyphæ, alien fungi and bacteria, for under such circumstances any intruder might be easily detected and ruthlessly destroyed. Nevertheless a few animals have managed to secure a foothold in the nests, but so far as known, only in those belonging to species of *Atta* s. str. and *Acromyrmex.* I have never seen any traces of myrmecophiles in the many nests of *Trachymyrmex, Mycetosorites* and *Cyphomyrmex* which I have examined. Bates (1892) and Brent (1886) state that certain Amphisbænian lizards manage to live in the *Atta* nests of Brazil and Trinidad. It is probable that these reptiles feed on the ants. Belt (1874) mentions a large *Staphylinid* beetle as occurring on the *Atta* nests of Nicaragua, and Wasmann (1900) concludes that this beetle, which he identifies as *Smilax pilosa* Fabr., is probably a true myrmecophile, because it so closely resembles the large *Atta* workers in its dark brown color and abundant pile. The same author (1894, 1895) mentions several Histerid beetles (*Philister rufulus* Lewis, *Hister* (?) *costatus* Mars, *Reninus salvini* Lewis and *Carcinops* (?) *multistriata* Lewis) as having been taken from the nests of *Atta mexicana*, and three Staphylinidæ belonging to the genera *Aleochara* and *Atheta* from the nests of *A. sexdens.* These are probably all not true guests but synœketes. To the same group belong also a number of specimens of the myriopod *Scutigera* which I found running about in the galleries of an *A. texana* nest.

The only myrmecophiles known to live in intimate relations with Attiine ants are the small and aberrant cockroaches of the genus *Attaphila* of which I described the first species (*A. fungicola*, Pl. LIII, Figs. 47–49) from Texas (1900). This insect, which is very common in the fungus gardens of *A. texana*, measures only 3–3.5 mm. in length. It is yellowish brown and has very small eyes, one-jointed cerci, and peculiar antennæ, consisting of a few cylindrical joints. The females are wingless, the males have vestigial tegmina and hind wings. The antennæ are always imperfect, their terminal joints having been bitten off, in all probability, while the ants are clipping the fungus mycelium. The structure of the remaining antennal joints is so unlike that of all other Blattidæ that *Attaphila* must be regarded as the type of a distinct subfamily, the Attaphilinæ. Since publishing my description of this singular insect, I have had an opportunity of observing it in artificial nests. It does not feed on the fungus hyphæ as I at first supposed, but mounts the backs of the large soldiers while they are stalking about the garden and licks their surfaces after the manner of some of the myrmecophiles of other ants, notably the little cricket *Myrmecophila nebrascensis,* the Staphylinid beetle *Oxysoma oberthueri,* and the guest ant *Leptothorax emersoni.*

In 1901 Bolivar described a second species of *Attaphila (A. bergi),* which

Fig. 16.   Nest craters of *Atta (Mœllerius) versicolor* Pergande in a sandy "draw" at Yucca, Arizona.   (Photograph by the author.)

was discovered many years ago by Berg in the nests of *Acromyrmex lundi* in Argentina and Uruguay. This species (Pl. LIII, Figs. 50–54) is very similar to the Texan form and it too, seems always to have multilated antennæ. According to Berg "it is found in the nest of the ants, sitting on the back, neck or even on the head of the sexual individuals (never on the neuters), and when these swarm forth during the spring or summer, it is also carried out of the nests, still attached to its host."

2. Atta (Mœllerius) versicolor *Pergande.*

This ant is unquestionably a Mexican species which enters the United States only along its southwestern frontier where it inhabits the arroyo bottoms in the most arid regions.   I have observed the typical form of the species only in two localities, at Tucson, Arizona, and at Yucca in the same state, a few miles east of the Californian boundary.   At Tucson several colonies were found in an arroyo near the Carnegie Desert Botanical Labora-

Fig. 17.   One of the craters of the group represented in the preceding figure, about ¼ natural size, showing the difference between the pellets brought up by the ants and the surrounding soil.   (Photograph by the author.)

tory where the soil was probably somewhat moist at a depth of several feet, but where the surface was very hard and dry and covered with typical desert plants such as the retama (*Parkinsonia*), the small acacia known as "cat-claw" or "uña de gato" (*Acacia greggi*), the Mexican grease-wood (*Covillœa tridentata*), the ocotillo (*Fouquiera splendens*) and several cacti (*Opuntia*). At Yucca the ants occur in similar arroyos bordered with the beautiful pod-willows (*Chilopsis saligna*) in the midst of a very hot, dry desert, studded with clumps of cañatilla (*Ephedra*), huge tree-like yuccas, and "allthorn" bushes (*Kœberlinia*).   In both localities the nests were surmounted by from one to a dozen craters, varying from 10–30 cm. in diameter, and of very elegant and regular structure (Figs. 16 and 17).   This was noticeably the case at Yucca, where the craters were built of the coarse, uniform sand of the arroyo bed.   The earth or sand of the crater walls was often of a different color from the surrounding surface, showing that it had been brought up

Fig. 18.   Small crater of *Atta* (*Mœllerius*) *versicolor* covered with leaves of grease wood (*Covillœa*) collected by the ants at Tucson, Arizona.   These leaves are also scattered along the path leading to the crater (upper right hand corner of figure).   (Photograph by the author.)

from a considerable depth.   The opening at the bottom of the crater was 2–3 cm. in diameter and was often closed with earth.   Even about the open craters no ants were to be seen during the intense heat of the day.   Between four and five o'clock in the afternoon, however, they were seen leaving the nests in files, and slowly moving towards some desert shrub in the neighbor-hood for the purpose of cutting and carrying home its leaves.   At Tucson some of the colonies were collecting the entire young and tender leaves of the "cat-claw," and had completely defoliated some of the bushes (Figs. 18 and 19). Other colonies were carrying in the small leathery leaves and yellow flowers of the grease-wood. Considerable quantities of these leaves had often been gathered and dropped along the path or on the craters, as shown in Fig. 18, and left to wither in the sun when the ants withdrew into their nests during the night or early morning hours.

The colonies were much smaller than those of *Atta texana*, although they

Fig. 19.   Acacia bush defoliated by *Atta* (*Mœllerius*) *versicolor* at Tucson, Arizona.   (Photograph by the author.)

comprised several hundred workers. These varied considerably in size, especially at Yucca. Dr. William Cannon, director of the Desert Laboratory, kindly assisted me in excavating one of the nests which had only a single crater. The entrance gallery, about 2 cm. in diameter broke up into a number of small anastomosing galleries just beneath the surface and these reunited to form a single gallery extending down into coarse, friable sand to a depth of about a meter and terminating in a single small chamber which contained a fungus garden about the size of a walnut. This garden was lying on the floor of the chamber and consisted of fine leaf-pulp covered with a brilliant white mycelium dotted with bromatia. No other chambers or galleries could be found, and as the nest contained only about one hundred workers, the colony must have been incipient or enfeebled by age or adverse conditions. As we had spent a great deal of time excavating this nest, and as the heat was intense, so intense, in fact, that it caused the gutta-percha plate-holders of my photographing outfit to soften and crumple, we could not command sufficient energy to excavate a larger and more typical nest. Unfortunately my stay of only a few hours at Yucca did not suffice for the exploration of one of the much finer nests of that locality. Judging from the single nest examined at Tucson, *Mœllerius versicolor* resembles most of the species of *Acromyrmex* described by Mœller, Tanner, von Ihering and Forel in having only a single chamber and garden.

My notes on the subsp. *chisosensis* are even more fragmentary. At Terlingua, Texas, in the Great Bend of the Rio Grande, I found a few dead workers of this form in a spider's web under a stone, but was quite unable to locate the nest from which they came. Judge O. W. Williams, however, brought me a number of fresh specimens from a nest in a dry arroyo at the foot of the Chisos Mountains some miles southeast of Terlingua. Both localities are in very arid deserts, riven with cañons, though the vegetation is of a different type from that of southern Arizona. The red quicksilver-bearing soil supports a sparse growth of the sotol (*Dasylirion texanum*), desert spurges (*Euphorbia antisyphilitica* and *Iatropha spathulata*) and lechugilla (*Agave lechugilla*), and the steep cañon walls are spangled with star-like resurrection plants (*Selaginella lepidophylla*) and xerophytic ferns. Such a region, with an annual rainfall of barely 25 cm., is certainly a remarkable environment for an ant compelled to subsist on fungi that can grow only in a humid atmosphere, an ant, moreover, belonging to a group which was probably first developed in the rain-forests of the tropics.

3.   Atta (Trachymyrmex) septentrionalis *McCook*.

The species of *Trachymyrmex* form small colonies of at most two or three hundred, and often of only a few dozen individuals, and are so timid and retiring in their habits that they are readily overlooked unless their nests happen to be numerous and close together. And even when numerous the nests are not often seen as their earth-works disintegrate and their entrances are kept closed during considerable periods of the year.

Our best known species, *T. septentrionalis*, is widely distributed over the Gulf and South Atlantic States, the var. *obscurior* ranging from central Texas to Florida and the typical form from Maryland to New Jersey. There are no observations to show that either of these forms extends equally far north in the Mississippi Valley. Mr. Wm. T. Davis has found the typical form as far north as the Raritan River in New Jersey and although he has hitherto failed to take it on Staten Island, it may yet be found in certain parts of Long Island. Both forms of the species have the same habits, although the southern variety often makes larger and more complicated nests and lives in larger colonies than the typical northern form, which is always more or less depauperate, like all ants at the limit of their geographical range. The following description, except in so far as it relates to the size and complexity of the nest, will apply to both forms of the species.

According to my observations, *T. septentrionalis*, even in widely separated localities, always occupies a very precise ethological station. I have never found it except in pure sand and in open woods. It is abundant in the post-oak woods of Texas, especially in the neighborhood of Milano and Monto-polis, wherever the red clay is replaced by sand, in the hummocks of Florida (Miami, Jacksonville) and the pine barrens of New Jersey (Lakehurst, Toms River, etc.). The plant associations in all of these localities have a common *facies* in that they always comprise several species of oaks and many other plants and animals peculiar to the Louisianian portion of the Austroriparian subprovince.

Externally the nest of *T. septentrionalis* is very unlike that of any other North American ant known to me. It consists of a little mound of sand varying from 10 to 20 cm. in diameter, and a few cm. in height, of an elliptical, round, or crescentic form and placed at a distance of 5 to 10 cm. from the entrance. The latter is circular and varies from 4 mm. to 1 cm. in diameter, and the gallery into which it leads invariably slopes so as to form an angle with the surface. The sandpile lies in front of the entrance. The external appearance of one of these nests is shown in Fig. 20, from a photograph taken at Lakehurst, where the sand is often covered with the needles, twigs and cones of *Pinus rigida* and *inops*. The subterranean portion of the nest consists of from one to three series of straight galleries alternating with more or less spherical chambers, so that it is possible to distinguish a simple and a racemose type. To the former belong the young nests of the var. *obscurior* and all the nests of the typical *septentrionalis*, whereas the racemose type seems to occur only in old and flourishing colonies of the southern variety.

In the table on page 749 are given the dimensions in cm. of the galleries and chambers of ten nests of *T. septentrionalis* var. *obscurior* examined in three localities about Austin, Texas, nests A to F being of the simple, and G to J of the racemose type. Diagrammatic sections of nests C, D, F, and G–J, drawn to scale, are represented in Pls. LI to LIII, Figs. 37–42, 45. The entrance gallery is called gallery I, that between chambers I and II, gallery II and so on. Of the two measurements recorded for each chamber, the first is the depth or vertical, the second the breadth or transverse diameter. The chambers are either spherical, or if one diameter exceeds the other, it is most frequently the transverse, so that the chambers are often oblately spheroidal. As the galleries enter and leave the chambers at opposite points on their roofs and floors, the globular cavities have the appearance of being strung on the galleries like beads on a string. The most frequent nests are those of the form A–C, comprising only two galleries and two chambers, and these are the only ones described by previous observers (Morris, McCook, Swingle, Forel). The entrance gallery is commonly a

Fig. 20.   Nest of *Atta* (*Trachymyrmex*) *septentrionalis* in pine barren near Lakehurst, New Jersey, about ½ natural size.   The circular entrance is in the middle of the figure; the excavated sand is dumped out in a heap in front of it (below).   (Photograph by the author.)

few cm. in length and the first chamber is very small (2.8 × 3.2 cm. on an average). These represent the whole of the nest dug by the mother queen while establishing her colony, the other chambers and galleries being added subsequently by the workers. The table and the figures show very clearly that the length of Gal. II and the size of Ch. II, greatly exceed the queen's excavations and are in turn surpassed by subsequent excavations (Gals. III–IV and Chs. III–V). Nests with three, four and five chambers, like D, E, and F, are rarely encountered. Of the last I have seen only a single example and this was peculiar in having Chs. III and IV deeper than broad.

Atta (Trachymyrmex) septentrionalis McCook

Nest	Gal. I	Ch. I	Gal. II	Ch. II	Gal. III	Ch. III	Gal. IV	Ch. IV	Gal. V	Ch. V	Total Depth.
A	2.5	2.5×3.2	7.7	7.7×7.7	—	—	—	—	—	—	20.4
B	3.8	3.8×4.5	7.7	6.4×6.4	—	—	—	—	—	—	21.7
C	5.	4.×4.	5.	6.5×6.5	—	—	—	—	—	—	20.5
D	2.5	1.9×2.	13.5	6.4×6.5	0.	6.5×10.3	15.3	2.5×3.8	—	—	22.3
E	3.	3.5×4.	1.8	3.8×5.	10.2	3.8×5.	12.7	12.8×12.	23.	6.4×7.8	55.6
F	1.3	1.3×1.3	11.4	2.5×2.5	2.5	7.8×3.8	—	—	—	—	72.1
G	2.5	3.8×5.	a. 11.4 / b. 2.5	a. 6.3×8. / b. 6.3×9.	5.	5.×6.4	—	—	—	—	25.1
H	2.5	2.2×2.2	a. 7.8 / b. 12.8	a. 5.×6.4 / b. 7.8×8.3	7.8	3.8×3.8	—	—	—	—	38.5
I	1.3	1.3×1.3	a. 12.8 / b. 7.8	a. 7.8×7.8 / b. 2.5×3.2	a. 6.4 / b. 5.1	b. 5.×7. / a. 5.×5.	12.6	7.7×8.9	—	—	46.7
J	—	—	a. 7.8 / b. 7.1 / c. 8.9	a. 6.4×6.4 / b. 7.×10.2 / c. 7.6×7.6	a. 5.1 / b. 2.5 / c. 7.6	b. 7.6×7.6 / c. 6.4×7.6	—	—	—	—	33.1
Ave.	2.7	2.8×3.2	7.9	6.0×6.7	5.5	5.6×6.3	13.5	7.6×8.2	23.	6.4×7.8	35.6

Nest D was unique in having Chs. II and III opening directly into each other. Nests of the simpler racemose type, like G, are more frequent than simple nests with as many as four and five chambers, like D and E. In nests G–I the second gallery sent off a branch terminating in a chamber of its own (Ch. IIa). The terminal chamber of nest H (Ch. III), like that of nest E (Ch. IV), was very small and obviously in process of being excavated by the ants. In nest I the insects had completed at least a portion of the gallery (Gal. IIIa) leading from Ch. II and the ants, had they been left undisturbed, would probably have widened its end into another chamber (Ch. IIIa). In nest J, the largest and most complicated of the series, not only did Gal. II form two branches, but one of these divided in turn, so that there were three galleries, each terminating in two chambers (Chs. II a, b, c, and Ch. III a, b, c) separated by a gallery (Gals. III a, b, c). Since in all of the nests the galleries formed an angle with the surface of the sand, their total depth, as given in the last column of the table, does not represent the vertical distance of the floor of the terminal chamber from the surface, but the oblique distance from the entrance. Both simple and racemose nests, moreover, though represented in the figures as lying in a single plane, are often bent, or, like nest I, of the latter type, radiate out from the entrance in three different intersecting planes.

When establishing their formicaries the ants select only those spots in the woods where the sand is permeated with fine rootlets. They are careful to leave these untouched, while hollowing out their chambers, as supports for their gardens, which in this, as in other species of *Trachymyrmex*, are always pendent and do not rest on the floor of the chamber like the gardens of *Atta* s. str., *Acromyrmex* and *Mœllerius*. The substratum on which the fungus is grown consists very largely of caterpillar excrement and withered oak-catkins, both picked up under the trees, but often small dead leaves or berries are used, and occasionally as Morris and McCook observed, flowers or green leaves are cut from the small herbaceous plants in the neighborhood. These substances are comminuted and placed on the pendent rootlets where they become knitted together by the rapidly proliferating fungus mycelium. The whole garden then hangs from the roof of the chamber as a cluster of nodular strands or plates separated from the walls and from one another by spaces sufficiently large to admit the ants to all parts of the structure. The first chamber, in which the original worker brood was reared by the queen, is often empty or has lying on its floor particles of exhausted vegetable substances ready to be carried out of the nest, or materials that have just been brought in. This chamber seems to be the work-shop in which the materials are prepared for insertion into the hanging gardens of the lower chambers. The appearance and arrangement of several of these gardens are shown in

Pls. LI–LIII, Figs. 30–46.   The mycelium in flourishing colonies has a bluish tint, somewhat like that of *Penicillium glaucum.* The hyphæ measure .78 *μ* in diameter.   The gongylidia are subspherical or pear-shaped, and average 4.5 *μ* in length and 3.6 *μ* in breadth, and are grouped in compact clusters or bromatia averaging .4–.5 mm. in diameter.

In Texas the most favorable time to study the nests of *T. obscurior* is during the month of April.   Then the ants are actively enlarging and deepening their nests and bringing in supplies for their gardens.   While excavating they advance in a small phalanx up the inclined entrance gallery, each laden with a cuboidal sand pellet about 2 mm. in diameter, walk slowly to the sand pile, deposit their burdens and then return for others.   The deälated females, of which there may be as many as four or five in a nest, toil in the

Fig. 21.   Brood of *Atta (Trachymyrmex) obscurior.*   About twice natural size.   Three packets of eggs are shown enveloped in fungus mycelium.   (Photograph by Mr. A. Beutenmüller.)

phalanx like the workers.   At the slightest alarm the ants immediately retreat into the nest and usually a single worker takes up her position in the entrance and holding a sand-pellet in her jaws, waits patiently till all danger has passed, before venturing forth and leading the troop of her sand-laden sisters.   When foraging the ants go out singly and in various directions, pick up what they can find and return with it to the nest, moving slowly and sedately over the sand.   The deälated females may also be seen in the act of carrying caterpillar droppings and leaves to the nest.   If rudely touched with the finger or a stick, the insect drops her burden, curls herself up, folds her legs and antennæ and "feigns death."   At such times her rough yellowish brown body is almost indistinguishable from the sand on which she lies.   When the nest is ruthlessly torn open, the ants, especially if they are numerous and have a large brood, do not feign death but boldly assail the intruder with their mandibles.

The nests remain in fine condition throughout May and the early part of June, while the young are being reared. The eggs are broadly elliptical and embedded in masses in pure white hyphæ. (Fig. 21.) These delicate vegetable strands serve to keep the eggs together, thus enabling the ants to carry them about in packets, afford an admirable protection and, as soon as the larvæ hatch, represent a supply of very accessible food. The older larvæ and young pupæ, however, are always free from adhering hyphæ, so that their surfaces are smooth and glistening, till they develop the rough, tuberculate integument of the adult stage. The brood is undoubtedly

Fig. 22. Nest of *Atta (Trachymyrmex) septentrionalis* var. *obscurior* in sandy post-oak wood near Delvalle, Texas. About ¼ natural size. This represents the condition of the nest during the dry summer. A few sticks and dead leaves cover the entrance just below the middle of the figure. (Photograph by Mr. C. G. Hartmann.)

moved from chamber to chamber to suit the varying conditions of heat and moisture. Throughout the warm days of May and June it is kept in the superficial apartments. On the morning of June 11, 1903, after an unusually cool night, I found the ants and entire brood of several nests huddled together in the lowermost chambers, but during the warm afternoon of the same day the young had been brought very near the surface. At Miami, Florida, the males and females were mature and ready for the nuptial flight as early as May 9; in Texas I have not seen them in this condition till the second week in June, and to judge from the date on the label of a winged female in my collection the sexual phases of the typical form do not mature in New Jersey till some time in August.

When its nest is disturbed, *T. septentrionalis,* like other Attii is very careful to rescue portions of its fungus gardens as well as its brood. A number of colonies, whose nests I had excavated in the post-oak woods at Montopolis, were found a few days later to have made new nests a few feet from the old sites and to have carried with them such fragments of their gardens as they could rescue. They had suspended these to the rootlets in one or two chambers which they had succeeded in excavating in the meantime, and were busy carrying in caterpillar excrement and withered oak catkins.

During the spring and autumn *T. septentrionalis* may be found abroad at all hours of the day, but with the growing heat of the summer it becomes increasingly crepuscular and nocturnal. And as soon as the dry weather sets in, it greatly contracts or completely closes with dead leaves and twigs the orifice of its nest to reduce or prevent the evaporation of the moisture from the chambers. The sandpile subsides under the influence of the elements till the nest becomes barely distinguishable from the surrounding leaf-strewn surface (Fig. 22). It is then almost impossible to find the nests even in localities where previous exploration has shown them to be very numerous. The ants no longer venture forth but spend all their time weeding and rearranging their gardens in the moist subterranean chambers. Immediately after the first warm rain, however, the nests are reopened, excavations and repairs to the chambers are renewed, the exhausted portions of the gardens are ejected and the ants sally forth in quest of fresh supplies.

4. Atta (Trachymyrmex) turrifex *Wheeler.*

As this species is even more timid and retiring than *T. septentrionalis,* it was some time before I learned to find its colonies and gained an acquaintance with its habits. Its geographical range covers the dry deserts of Trans Pecos Texas, and slightly overlaps the range of *septentrionalis* along the escarpment of the Edwards Plateau in the central portion of the state. That it is a more adaptable ant than its eastern and northern congener, is shown by its occurrence in the following diverse stations:

1. In the treeless deserts at Del Rio, Langtry, Marfa, Alpine and Ft. Stockton, in dry stony soil fully exposed to the glare of the sun. In these localities the colonies are widely scattered.

2. In the clayey soil of the post-oak woods and "cedar-brakes" (*Juniperus sabinoides*) near Austin (Fig. 23), along the Perdenales River, and at Marble Falls. Here the colonies are often numerous and close together.

3. In the pure sand of open fields at Montopolis on the Colorado River. In this locality the colonies are infrequent and mingled with those of *sep-*

Fig. 23. "Cedar Brake" (*Juniperus sabinoides*) near Austin, Texas. Home of *Atta* (*Trachymyrmex*) *turrifex*. (Photograph by Prof. W. L. Bray.)

tentrionalis, a condition which also obtains in sandy portions of the post-oak woods.

Though structurally closely resembling the eastern species, *T. turrifex* may be readily distinguished by a number of ethological characters. Its colonies are much smaller, often consisting of only two or three dozen individuals. Nevertheless a single nest may contain as many as four or five deälated females. The nesting habits are most conveniently studied in the post-oak woods, where the ants prefer to live in the shade of the trees. Here the red clay is overlaid with a stratum of less compact black soil two or three decimeters deep. The external structure of the nest is very different from

Fig. 24.   Turret-shaped entrance to nest of *Atta* (*Trachymyrmex*) *turrifex* in a cedar brake near Austin, Texas.   (Photograph by Mr. A. L. Melander.)

that of *septentrionalis.* The orifice is only 3–4 mm. in diameter and in typical nests, does not open on the surface of the soil but at the top of a cylindrical turret or chimney about 10 mm. in diameter and from 10–40 mm. high. The walls of this turret, which are made of earth particles, small juniper twigs and other vegetable débris (Fig. 24) are sufficiently resistant to withstand heavy showers. As the nests are often located on sloping ground the turret would seem to be an ingenious adaptation for keeping the water from entering the subterranean galleries and chambers. Occasionally I have found nests with abnormal turrets, like the one represented in Pl. L, Fig. 27, which has the summit enlarged and spreading and provided with three distinct orifices. The pellets of earth brought up by the ants are cuboidal or polyhedral, of uniform size and measure about 2 mm. in diameter. They are not cast to one side as in *septentrionalis* but in a closed circle at a distance of 8–12 cm. from the entrance. As this circle grows in height it forms a very shallow crater with the turret rising abruptly in its center. In the post-oak woods and cedar-brakes the castings are red or dull vermilion and contrast strongly with the black soil or dead leaves of the surface.

The galleries and chambers alternate with one another as in the simple type of *septentrionalis* nests, but the chambers are smaller and the galleries are much longer and usually descend vertically into the soil. These differences are distinctly shown in the figures (Pl. LI, Figs. 33–36) and in the measurements (in cm.) of the accompanying table.

Atta (Trachymyrmex) turrifex Wheeler.

Nest	Gal. I	Ch. I	Gal. II	Ch. II	Gal. III	Ch. III	Gal. IV	Ch. IV	Gal. V	Ch. V	Total Depth
K	3.7	1.8×1.8	4.2	1.8×2.5	5.	3.8×3.8	6.3	4. ×4.2	7.7	——	38.3
L	1.8	1.3×1.3	8.2	2.8×2.8	9.5	.4×6.5	13.4	3.2×6.5	17.4	4.5×3.8	66.1
M	2.5	.8×1.	11.5	3.2×3.2	14.6	4.2×6.4	15.3	5. ×5.	—	——	57.1
N	3.6	1.3×1.8	6.5	3.5×3.8	11.5	3.8×7.6	7.5	1.5×1.5	—	——	39.2
O	3.6	1.3×1.3	2.5	2.5×5.	12.8	5. ×6.4	7.5	5.2×7.5	—	——	40.4
P	3.8	2.5×2.5	1.5	2.5×3.8	6.3	4. ×5.2	9.	4. ×6.5	10.5	6.5×7.8	50.6
Q	3.5	2.5×2.5	5.	4. ×4.	18.	2. ×2.5	16.5	3.5×5.	15.	——	70.
R	10.2	2. ×2.	23.	5. ×6.4	19.	2.5×3.8	30.5	6.5×7.8	8.	3.8×3.8	110.5
Ave.	4.1	1.7×1.7	7.8	3.8×3.9	12.	3.6×5.2	13.2	4.1×5.5	11.7	4.9×5.1	59.0

All of these nests were located in the clayey soil of the post-oak woods except the last (R) which was in pure sand. Owing to the length of its galleries, this is exceptional in its total depth (110.5 cm.), and therefore abnormally increases the average length of the galleries I to V in the table. The average depth of nests K to Q is only 50.8 cm. which is less than half the depth of nest R. The nests usually comprise four chambers (Fig. 25), but five are often met with, and here, as in *septentrionalis,* the galleries and chambers have their dimensions suddenly increased, below the first chamber, which is the work of the mother queen. I have seen but one *turrifex* nest that resembled the racemose type of *septentrionalis* in having two branches to Gal. IV, each terminating in a chamber. Comparing the nests of the two species we see that both start with the simple, primitive type consisting of alternating galleries and chambers and that *turrifex* continues its excavations according to this pattern, whereas flourishing colonies of *septentrionalis* change to the racemose type which bears an unmistakable resemblance to the nests of *Atta* s. str.

The greater length of the *turrifex* galleries in pure sand is undoubtedly

Fig. 25.   Section of nest of *Atta* (*Trachymyrmex*) *turrifex* showing four chambers exposed (at points of paper triangles numbered 1 to 4).   About ¼ natural size.   (Photograph by Mr. C. G. Hartmann.)

due to the need of reaching a stratum of greater dampness.   In the dry Trans Pecos deserts the same tendency is observable.   In that region I repeatedly endeavored to excavate nests, but was never able to reach the chambers on account of the extreme hardness of the stony soil.   I am convinced, however, that these nests were more than a meter deep. That *T. turrifex* requires rather moist soil is also shown by a peculiarity of its nests in the post-oak regions. Here, as I have said, the subsoil is red clay overlaid with a dryer, and more porous black earth. The ants not only carry their excavations down into the subsoil but carefully line the galleries and chambers in the black soil, to the very orifice of the turret, with a thin layer of clay brought up from below. Thus the nest becomes a bottle with thin clay walls, alternately constricted into slender tubes (the galleries) and dilated into ampulliform enlargements (the chambers). This clay lining is probably a very efficient means of preventing both the escape of the moisture from the chambers during dry spells and the entrance during rainy weather of too much moisture from the soil. Unlike the nests of *septentrionalis*, those of *turrifex* are not closed during the dry season. Such closure is in fact unnecessary because the nests are considerably deeper, situated in soil which retains the moisture much longer, and have very small orifices.

The first chamber, like that of the *septentrionalis* nest, is used as a workshop and temporary repository for fresh and discarded vegetable substances. The rootlets of plants are also left dangling into the remaining chambers as a suspensorium for the fungus gardens. These resemble the gardens of *septentrionalis* but are smaller, whiter, and of a more delicate texture, as if the vegetable substratum on which they were grown had been more finely comminuted. In the confection of this substratum the same materials are used, viz., the withered catkins of oaks, the scales of buds, bits of dead leaves and the excrement of caterpillars. I have never seen these ants cutting or bringing in green leaves of any description. At Marfa and Ft. Stockton they were collecting the withered florets of a small yellow composite (*Pectis tenella*). The nest openings were often surrounded by a circlet of these florets, so that to one riding over the desert each nest seemed to be marked by a small handful of saffron. All of the vegetable substances are picked up by the ants from the ground and not collected directly from the plants, as *turrifex* is even less inclined than *septentrionalis* to climb about on the vegetation. The microscopic structure of the fungus gardens is very much like that of *septentrionalis*. The hyphæ measure .78 μ in diameter; the bromatia .3–.4 mm. and consist of beautifully developed gongylidia 3.5–4.7 μ in length and somewhat less in breadth.

The deälated females of *turrifex* take part in excavating and foraging, like the workers. On one occasion, early in the morning of June 14, in the midst of the desert at Marfa, I came upon a whole colony of this ant, comprising some thirty workers and five deälated females, in the act of digging a nest in the hard adobe soil. They had evidently been compelled to forsake their old nest during the night on account of the drought, which was almost unprecedented even in that region, as it had not rained for nine months. As I have also found many abandoned nests of this ant in the cedar brakes about Austin, I infer that it not infrequently migrates to more favorable spots. It would be interesting to know whether on such occasions the old queens carry over to the new quarters portions of the fungus gardens in their hypopharyngeal pocket, or whether the workers transfer the old gardens piece-meal during the cool night hours. The latter would seem to be the more probable procedure.

T. *turrifex* is, if anything, slower and more sedate in its movements than *septentrionalis*. It also "feigns death" more readily and never seems to resent the destruction of its nest. Only a few workers are seen at any one time outside the nest. The slightest disturbance causes these to withdraw into the turret, and one may sit motionless near the nest for many minutes before they muster sufficient courage to venture forth again. When several of these ants, together with pieces of their gardens, were placed in a dish with a number of *septentrionalis* workers, a conflict ensued, in which the latter were the aggressors and came off victorious. They carried the *turrifex* garden piece by piece into a wide chamber they had excavated in some sand at the bottom of the dish, but by the following morning they had thrown it all out again and, although they had been without food for several days, they would have nothing to do with it.

The breeding season of *turrifex* must come later in the summer than that of *septentrionalis*. During early June I found a few young larvæ in the nests of the former species, but the only winged female I have seen was captured in flight by Mr. W. H. Long on September 27. I have never been able to obtain a male of this species.

5. Atta (Trachymyrmex) jamaicensis *Ern. André.*

Like the preceding two species of *Trachymyrmex*, T. *jamaicensis*, though confined to the West Indies, occurs only in association with a xerophytic flora. It is a larger, much darker ant, with unusually long legs and antennæ. I found it first in the Bahamas, on both Andros and New Providence Islands. On the former it was seen wherever I landed and searched for it — at Big Wood Key, Mangrove Key, on several of the uncharted keys along the course of the Southern Bight and about Crawl Creek. On New Providence it was found in the neighborhood of Fort Charlotte. It prefers to nest in the pure white foraminiferous sand of the sea-beach, at or just above high water mark, along the edges of the 'coppets' which consist very largely of coarse grasses, sea-grape, cocoa-plum, wild sapodilla, sea-lavender and palmettos. Its nest, which is most readily found by tracking foraging workers, is surmounted by a very flat and obscure crater about 30 cm. in diameter with an oblique and somewhat eccentric orifice 5–10 mm. in diameter. The ants collect buds, small flowers, bits of dead and living leaves and caterpillar excrement as a substratum for their fungus gardens. When rudely touched the workers fall over and "feign death." At first I was inclined to believe that this species is restricted to the sandy seabeaches, but on walking inland about two miles from All Saint's Rectory at Mangrove Key, I found it nesting also in clearings among the 'coppets' wherever a small amount of rich black soil in the cavities of the rough Æolian limestone had induced the negroes to plant maize and other vegetables. Here the ants were busily engaged in cutting and carrying into their nests bits of the green maize leaves after the manner of the species of *Atta* s. str. In other places, like Fort Charlotte, on New Providence Island, the ants were nesting in the dry shady 'coppets.' In all of these localities the nests extended down through holes or crevices in the limestone, so that I was unable to obtain a satisfactory conception of their structure.

On a recent trip to the Island of Culebra, a few miles east of Porto Rico, I again encountered this ant but under conditions more favorable for study. The vegetation on Culebra, which is too low to intercept the rain-laden trade winds from the Atlantic, is decidedly xerophytic. There is no standing water on the island and the short arroyos dry up very soon after a shower. A number of colonies of *T. jamaicensis* were found in the shade of the trees on the banks of these arroyos. The colonies, at the time of my visit (March 2–9), were in an opulent condition and each comprised numerous larvæ, pupæ and winged males and females in addition to about a hundred workers. Externally the nests, though in black friable soil, were like those on the sandy beaches of the Bahamas. Their subterranean structure closely resembled that of the simplest, two-chambered nests of *septentrionalis*. The entrance descended into the soil obliquely and at a distance of 2–3 cm. below the surface, widened into a small spherical chamber 2.5 cm. in diameter. This chamber contained no fungus garden but only a few workers apparently engaged in comminuting leaf clippings and caterpillar excrement. A second gallery 5–10 cm. in length led off obliquely from the bottom of this chamber and terminated in a larger spheroidal cavity 6.5–9 cm. in diameter, filled with a flourishing fungus garden of coarse and nodular structure and suspended from rootlets. The brood, callow and recently matured sexual forms were ensconced among the pendent folds and strands. The mycelium was of a bluish color, like that of *septentrionalis*, with hyphæ .58 μ in diameter. The bromatia measured .36 mm. and consisted of well-developed pyriform gongylidia 4–4.6 μ long and 1.5–3 μ broad.

6. Atta (**Mycetosoritis**) hartmanni sp. nov.

This interesting little ant was discovered May 9, 1903, in the sandy country on the left bank of the Colorado River at Montopolis and Delvalle, near Austin, Texas, while, with the assistance of Mr. C. G. Hartmann, I was examining and photographing the nests of *Trachymyrmex turrifex* and *septentrionalis.* At first I was inclined to regard the diminutive workers as merely belonging to incipient *Trachymyrmex* colonies, but closer study soon showed that these little ants were not only specifically distinct but also represented a new and interesting subgenus, in certain respects intermediate between *Trachymyrmex* and *Cyphomyrmex.* There were hundreds of their nests, often within a few decimeters of one another, in the fields or in clearings among the oaks and wherever the sand was fully exposed to the sun. These regions were also inhabited by several species of solitary wasps

Fig. 26.   Crater of *Atta* (*Mycetosoritis*) *hartmanni* from sandy post-oak woods at Montopolis, Texas.   Natural size.   (Photograph by Mr. C. G. Hartmann.)

(*Microbembex* and *Pompilus*) and numerous colonies of ants (*Trachymyrmex turrifex* and *septentrionalis, Aphænogaster treatæ, Pheidole splendidula* and *morrisi, Solenopsis geminata, Pogonomyrmex comanche, Prenolepis arenivaga,* etc.). The herbaceous flora of the region consisted of a sparse growth of bull-nettles (*Iatropha stimulosa*), showy gaillardia (*Gaillardia pulchella*), butterfly wēed (*Asclepias tuberosa*), white prickly poppy (*Argemone alba*), stone crop (*Sedum*) and cactus (*Opuntia engelmanni*), all in full bloom.

The nests of the *Mycetosoritis* are small turriform craters of pure sand 5–8 cm. in diameter at the base and tapering rapidly to the summit, which is 2.5–4 cm. high and perforated with a circular orifice barely 2 mm. in diameter (Fig. 26). Occasionally the summit is double (Pl. L, Fig. 28) and furnished with two entrances, which, however, soon unite to form a single gallery. The internal structure of the nest resembles on a small scale that of *Trachymyrmex turrifex.* It consists of from two to four alternating vertical galleries and spheroidal chambers. As the former are very tenuous and run through pure sand, the excavation of the nests is rather

Fig. 27.   Section of nest of *Atta* (*Mycetosoritis*) *hartmanni* in pure sand at Delvalle, Texas. About ⅛ natural size.   (Photograph by Mr. C. G. Hartmann.)

difficult. The measurements of six of these nests (S to X) are given in the accompanying table, diagrams of three of them are represented in Figs. 30–32, Pl. LI, and photographs of portions of one of them in Figs. 27 and 28.

Atta (*Mycetosorites*) *hartmanni* sp. nov.

Nest	Gal. I	Ch. I	Gal. II	Ch. II	Gal. III	Ch. III	Gal. IV	Ch. IV	Total Depth
S.	5.	2. ×2.5	15.	2.6×4.	—	——	—	——	24.6
T.	6.3	1.3×2.	20.5	2.5×4.	18.5	2.5×3.4	—	——	51.6
U.	5.	1.4×1.4	13.	2.5×4.	29.4	2.5×4.5	—	——	53.4
V.	7.6	1.3×1.3	13.3	3.3×3.8	7.	4. ×4.	—	——	36.5
W.	6.	1.2×1.3	18.7	2.3×3.7	20.	2.9×4.1	14	2.×3.4	67.1
X.	5.2	.8×1.5	28.	1. ×3.2	25.3	2.5×4.5	14	2.×3.4	78.8
Ave.	6.5	1.3×1.6	18.1	2.3×3.8	19.8	2.8×4.1	14	2.×3.4	52.1

The galleries are proportionally longer than those of *turrifex* nests in clay or black soil, and the chambers are absolutely smaller and more oblately

Fig. 28. One of the pendent fungus gardens of the nest shown in the preceding figure, slightly enlarged. (Photograph by Mr. C. G. Hartmann.)

spheroidal. On an average, however, the *Mycetosoritis* nests are quite as deep (55.1 cm). Their resemblance to *turrifex* nests in pure sand, like nest

R of the table on p. 756, is greater owing to the elongation of the galleries of the latter species.

Like the species of *Trachymyrmex, M. hartmanni* leaves the rootlets dangling into the chambers as suspensoria for its fungus-gardens (Fig. 28). These gardens, however, have a much more delicate and flocculent texture and are made up almost exclusively of the anthers of plants, knit together by a snow-white mycelium consisting of slender hyphæ .58 μ in diameter. The bromatia, which measure .3–.4 mm. consist of typical pyriform gongylidia 1.5–4.3 μ in length and 1.3–4 μ in breadth.

The colonies are small, not exceeding 60 to 70 workers. Only a single deälated female was found in each of the nests. I was unable to find any

Fig. 29. Fungus garden of *Atta (Mycetosoritis) hartmanni*, removed from the nest intact and placed on the ground. (Photograph by Mr. C. G. Hartmann.)

larvæ or pupæ. Mr. A. M. Ferguson, who helped me excavate a number of the nests on one occasion, and kept the ants with some of their gardens in an artificial nest, succeeded later in the summer in rearing the males and winged females described on pp. 715–716. The workers are extremely timid and "feign death" with the utmost readiness. Their small rough bodies are then quite indistinguishable from the sand grains among which they lie. Only a few workers forage or excavate at a time. They seek the withered anthers where they have fallen or have been drifted by the wind on the surface of the sand and slowly and laboriously transport them to their nests. These anthers, many of which still contain pollen grains, are inserted entire in the gardens and are evidently responsible for the light and flocculent

texture. Exposure of only a few moments to the air causes the delicate
mycelium to wither and contract. The garden of the chamber represented
in Fig. 28 was thus dried, but the one in Fig. 29 was photographed immediately after its removal from the nest. The ants appear to be crepuscular
or nocturnal. I have not seen them at work after ten o'clock in the morning
except on very cloudy days.

On June 5, when I paid a second visit to the sandy country at Montopolis and Delvalle, all the nests were closed and the craters revealed no signs
of recent excavation. They had merely crumbled, marking the sites of the
nests as obscure little piles of sand. I opened several of the nests and found
the workers moving diligently about in their gardens, which were in fine
condition. On June 26, when, just before leaving Texas, I paid a final
visit to the dry post-oak woods, not a trace of the nests could be found.
The wind and rain had completely obliterated the fragile turrets and fused
their sandgrains with the surrounding surface, so that even the closest
observer would never have suspected the existence of innumerable colonies
of little ants diligently cultivating their hanging gardens in the dark bosom
of the yellow sands.

The foregoing description of the nests of *Mycetosoritis* shows that this
ant is closely related to *Trachymyrmex*. The members of the genus *Cyphomyrmex*, as will be seen from the following accounts of two species have
very different habits.

7. Cyphomyrmex wheeleri *Forel.*

This species appears to be more widely distributed than most of the
preceding, since it ranges from Central Texas to California and probably
also over a large portion of northern Mexico. In Texas it is rather rare
and, according to my observations, occurs only in arid regions, especially
on the Edwards Plateau and Grand Prairie and in the stony deserts of the
Trans Pecos country about Langtry and Fort Davis. Although several
of the preceding Attii prefer to live in dry localities among plant associations
of a more or less xerophytic habitus, the abode of *C. wheeleri* is characterized
by even greater aridity. Most of my observations on the habits of this ant
were made among the lime-stone hills of the plateau escarpment just west
of Austin. Some of these hills, which are often beautifully stratified and
terraced and belong to lower cretaceous formations, are shown in Fig. 30,
from a photograph taken in the early morning when the long shadows
accentuate their peculiar structure. The terraced slopes are strewn with
blocks of limestone of different sizes. Among these hills, from early spring
to late autumn, the heat and the glare of the sun reflected from the white

Fig. 30.   Limestone hills of the Edwards Plateau, near Austin, Texas,   Home of *Cyphomyrmex wheeleri*.   (Photograph by Prof. W. L. Bray.)

rock are exceedingly oppressive. Water is very scarce and the vegetation is so sparse and stunted or of such a xerophytic character as to yield little shade except in the deeper cañons. The trees and shrubs comprise such species as the mountain cedar (*Juniperus sabinoides*), several hackberries (*Celtis helleri, reticulata* and *pallida,*) oaks (*Quercus fusiformis breviloba* and *schneckii*), buckeyes (*Ungnadia speciosa* and *Æsculus octandra*), dwarf mulberry (*Morus celtidifolia*), dwarf walnut (*Juglans rupestris*), frijolillo, or coral bean (*Sophora secundiflora*), Texas persimmon (*Brayodendron texanum*), madroña (*Arbutus xalapensis* var. *texana*), algerita (*Berberis trifoliata*), *Eysenhardtia amorphoides, Leucophyllum texanum, Rhus microphylla* and *virens,* and *Ephedra antisyphilitica.* During the spring the bare rocks are beautiful with a profusion of smaller plants (*Gilia rigidula, Castilleia, Salvia texana, Stillingia angustifolia, Palafoxia texana, Androstephium violaceum, Camassia fraseri, Yucca rupicola* and *Nolina*)

It is only on the higher and more arid terraces that *C. wheeleri* manages to live and cultivate its fungus gardens, where long after other plants have bloomed and deep into the winter the golden heads of *Actinella scaposa* nod on their long stems. The nests are always under large stones covering a little lingering moisture in the hard soil, which consists very largely of disintegrated limestone. Each colony comprises only a few dozen workers and a single deälated female except during the spring and early summer, when one finds also several callow workers, males and females and a variable number of eggs, larvæ and pupæ. The workers are nocturnal, at least during the warm seasons of the year, a peculiarity which is indicated by their yellow color. They are very slow in their movements and readily "feign death."

The excavations though extensive for such small ants, are unlike those of *Atta, Trachymyrmex* and *Mycetosoritis.* A few rough and occasionally branching galleries about 1–2 cm. in diameter run along the surface covered by the stone, and descend vertically into the ground to a depth of 10–15 cm. One of the surface galleries terminates in a small entrance at the edge of the stone where its opening may be marked by a small crater. Irregular and indistinct dilatations in the galleries represent the chambers of other Attii, and in one of these dilatations, which is often fully exposed when the stone is removed, or may be readily uncovered at a depth of a few cm., the single fungus garden is found. This rests directly on the ground and is spheroidal or ovate, usually about the size of a filbert or pecan nut, more rarely half as large as a hen's egg. It consists of a delicate flocculent substratum made of small vegetable slivers covered with a dense snow white mycelium. The slivers average from 1–3 mm. in length and appear to have been torn from the stems of herbaceous plants. They undergo no trituration or comminution before they are inserted in the garden. The mycelium which binds these slivers together bears distinct bromatia .6–.7 mm. in diameter and consisting of pear-shaped gongylidia 1.5–3.5 μ in length and .78–1.56 μ broad. They are less globose than the gongylidia of *Atta* and *Trachymyrmex* and less club-shaped than those of the South American species of *Cyphomyrmex* represented in Mœller's figures. Sometimes as in these species, however, they are not terminal but appear as mere swellings in the course of the hyphæ. The brood is embedded in the fungus gardens and the eggs and young larvæ and often also the older larvæ and pupæ are covered with a delicate film of mycelium.

The ants carry all the exhausted particles of the substratum out of the galleries and build them into a flat mass which adheres to the lower surface of the stone. More rarely this refuse is dumped outside the entrance of the nest at the edge of the stone. As the mass of slivers is sometimes nearly as large as a man's hand and therefore greatly exceeds the size of the flourishing gardens, one is compelled to conclude that the vegetable particles contain but little available nutriment for the fungus and have to be continually renewed by the workers. Moreover, as these masses of exhausted substratum are often found under stones covering completely deserted galleries, it is probable that the ants keep moving to new nesting sites. This moving must be necessitated by the small amount of moisture in the soil and the rapidity with which it evaporates even from under large stones.

In the vicinity of Austin, *C. wheeleri* is not confined to the limestone hills of the Edwards Plateau. On three occasions I found small isolated crater nests of this species in the hard pebbly soil of the open woods at a lower altitude in the outskirts of the town. The exhausted substratum was dumped to one side of the small circular entrance which descended vertically into the soil. These nests must have been much deeper than the ones above described as I never succeeded in excavating them completely or in finding the fungus garden.

The males and winged females were found in the nests on the Edwards Plateau June 26th, and as early as June 8th in the somewhat warmer country about Fort Davis. In the latter locality I noticed among the vegetable slivers of the exhausted substratum a number of elytra, thoraces, etc., of small beetles, but whether these insects had been collected for food or merely formed a part of the substratum, I am unable to say.

8.   **Cyphomyrmex rimosus** *Spinola.*

The stations inhabited by the various subspecies and varieties of this widely distributed ant afford a striking contrast with the arid environment of *C. wheeleri* and entail a corresponding contrast in habits. All the forms of *rimosus* that have come under my observation live in the shade of trees and bushes in rather moist, black soil. These ants are, in fact, restricted to such localities on account of the material they require for constructing their gardens and the peculiarities of the fungus which they cultivate. The habits of the subspecies *minutus* which I have had abundant opportunities of observing in the Florida Keys, Bahamas, Culebra and Porto Rico, and those of the subspecies *dentatus* which I first found in the lovely barrancas about Cuernavaca, Mexico, resemble so closely the habits of the var. *comalensis* at New Braunfels, Texas, that I may confine my remarks very largely to this form.

At New Braunfels a number of beautiful springs, the sources of the Comal River, gush forth from the foot of Mission Mountain, one of the limestone hills that constitute the Grand Prairie escarpment (Fig. 31). The volume and temperature of these springs is practically constant during the entire year. They nourish an exuberant vegetation consisting of ash-trees, live-oaks and shittim wood (*Bumelia lycioides*) and a dense undergrowth of subtropical shrubs and herbaceous plants too numerous to mention. The entomologist who enters this undergrowth must be prepared to endure the fiery torments of the "red-bugs" or "coloradillos" ("*Leptus*" *irritans*) and exercise some care lest he tread on a water moccasin. But, if he be in search of ants he will be rewarded by finding a number of interesting subtropical species, among others three species of *Pseudomyrma* (*pallida, brunnea* and *flavida*), a singular little *Strumigenys* (*S. margaritæ* Forel) hitherto known only from the island of St. Vincent, besides the fungus-growing ant with which we are here concerned.

This ant, owing to the close agreement between its color and the black soil over which it moves, is more difficult to detect than any of the other small Attii described in the preceding pages. Single workers wander about slowly in the damp shade of the plants in search of the caterpillar excrement with which they construct their gardens. As soon as one of the short, cylindrical, ribbed pellets is found, the ant seizes it in her jaws, raises it above her head like a man shouldering a cask and returns home with accelerated pace. The slightest touch causes the ant to drop her load, draw up her legs and antennæ and "feign death." And he must have exceptionally good eye-sight who can distinguish her rough, opaque and inert body from the particles of earth among which it falls.

The colonies of *C. comalensis* are larger than those of *C. wheeleri*, sometimes comprising a hundred or more workers and from one to three deälated queens. The nests are under rather small flat stones or pieces of wood, with the entrance sometimes nearly a cm. in diameter, at the periphery. On

Fig. 31. One of the sources of the Comal River at New Braunfels, Texas. Home of *Cyphomyrmex rimosus* var. *comalensis*. (Photograph by Prof. W. L. Bray.)

removing the stone or piece of wood the galleries are seen to be very irregular, running along the surface as in the nests of *C. wheeleri* and extending down into the soil to a depth of 20 to 35 cm. They adapt their course to the many small fragments of limestone on or below the surface. The single fungus garden, of irregularly flattened or sometimes of elongate and straggling form lies in dilated portions of the gallery, usually completely exposed by the removal of the stone. In many nests the garden rests on a small stone, piece of bark or dead leaf from which the earth has been carefully removed by the ants. So different is this garden from that of the other Attii heretofore described that it has been completely overlooked by all previous observers. The substratum consists of a mass of caterpillar droppings a few cm. in diameter, which have undergone so little manipulation by the ants that the individual pellets may be distinctly recognized even to the peculiar ridges produced by the rectal folds of the caterpillars.

The fungus grown on this substratum is not a mycelium as in all the species above described, but is in the form of a number of isolated whitish or yellowish bodies .25–.55 mm. in diameter, of the appearance and consistency of cheese crumbs and of an irregularly polygonal or pyriform shape (Pl. L, Fig. 29). Each of these bodies may be said to correspond to a cluster of gongylidia and may therefore be called a bromatium. It rests with one of its angles or surfaces on the caterpillar excrement, but no rhizoids or mycelial threads can be seen at this point entering and ramifying in the substratum. The whole garden is kept so moist that when first exposed to the air the surface glistens with a film of greenish liquid. As the bromatia rest on this liquid, which evidently represents a thick solution of fecal and vegetable substances, they are in a position to absorb nutriment directly. It is probable that the habit of placing the excrement on the surface of a small stone, bit of wood or dead leaf which happens to be found in the gallery of the nest, is for the purpose of retaining this nutrient moisture and preventing its absorption by the soil. All of these conditions are such as to restrict *C. comalensis* and the other forms of *rimosus* to moist, shady localities. Such situations are of course, also the only ones in which tropical and subtropical plants are sufficiently abundant to furnish an unfailing supply of caterpillar droppings.

When the bromatia are crushed and examined in water under a high power of the microscope, they are seen to consist of a dense mass of elliptical or subspherical cells measuring .78–2 μ in length and .78–1 μ in breadth. Among these there are also cells of other shapes and even smaller sizes as shown in Pl. LII, Fig. 43. The cytoplasm of all of these cells is colorless and finely granular and contains one or more clear vacuoles and a few small refractive corpuscles. A nucleus is probably present, but I have been unable to find it in my preparations. The cell wall is always very thin and transparent. These cells closely resemble those of the common yeast (*Saccharomyces*) except that they are considerably larger. Like the yeast cells they may often be found in the act of budding or dividing. In this manner probably arise the minute cells scattered about among those of much larger dimensions. All the cells are held together in the bromatial mass merely by cohesion of their surfaces without assuming polyhedral shapes from mutual pressure, and there is no perceptible intercellular substance nor any trace of an envelope enclosing the mass as a whole.

Neither the mycologists with whom I am acquainted nor the botanical works to which I have access, have given me any satisfactory information concerning the natural affinities of this singular fungus. That it must be in a purely vegetative stage of growth will probably be admitted, since there is nothing to suggest sporulation in the structure of the bromatia or the cells of which they consist. It is also evident that this plant must represent an entirely different fungus from any of those described by Mœller. Its cultivation on some artificial medium, such as agar mixed with sterilized extract of caterpillar excrement, may be expected to throw light on its affinities and to show that it belongs to some well known genus or species, but this can be undertaken only by a trained mycologist. It will be a long time, however, before we are in possession of any information in regard to these matters, if botanists continue to manifest as little interest in the fungi cultivated by ants as has been the case during the past fifteen years. In the meantime the singular fungus cultivated by *C. comalensis* and the other forms of *rimosus* over such an extensive area of the American tropics certainly deserves a name, and even at the risk of creating a synonym, I propose to call it *Tyridiomyces formicarum* gen. et sp. nov. and to assign it provisionally to the order Exoaceæ, a group which also includes the well-known yeast fungi.

I have proved that the ants eat the *Tyridiomyces*, by observing their behavior in artificial nests. On several occasions colonies were brought from New Braunfels to Austin, where they were kept in Petri dishes for periods of from one to four weeks and provided with the excrement of caterpillars (*Hyperchiria io*) which feed on the leaves of the southern hackberry (*Celtis mississippiensis*). The captive ants were as careful of the bromatia as of their brood. When the garden was disturbed they rearranged the pellets of excrement and deftly replaced the scattered and detached fungus bodies. Workers, females and males were frequently seen holding these bodies between their forelegs and eagerly rasping off portions of them with their tongues. Sometimes an ant would consume a whole bromatium, but more frequently only a portion was eaten. The irregular polygonal shape of the bodies is undoubtedly due to this method of feeding. It is equally certain that these bodies keep growing in size and regenerating the consumed portions by a rapid proliferation of their component cells. Caterpillar excrement freshly introduced into the nest was "seeded" by the workers either with entire bromatia brought from older portions of the garden or with small pieces bitten off from the bromatia and sprinkled over the new substratum. In the artificial nests the ants were unable to raise sufficient fungi for their consumption, so that in the course of a few weeks they devoured all of the bromatia and eventually died of starvation. As a rule the substratum employed by *C. comalensis* and the other forms of *rimosus*, that have come under my observation, consists exclusively of caterpillar droppings, but in several of the nests of the subspecies *minutus* in the island of Culebra, I also found small pieces of plant substances which I was unable to identify and a few small decomposing insect larvæ. These were mingled with the caterpillar excrement and also dotted with flourishing bromatia.

On one of my artificial nests of *comalensis* I made an observation which proves that this ant can also eat animal food. Several of the larvæ and pupæ that had been injured while the colony was being captured were eaten with avidity not only by the workers but also by the males and winged females. They did not, however, eat other insects, such as flies and small beetles, which I placed in their nest. The remains of the larvæ and pupæ were eventually inserted among the caterpillar excrement and carefully seeded with pieces of bromatia. This would seem to indicate that the beetle fragments seen in the nests of *C. wheeleri* at Fort Davis may have been similarly employed as a portion of the substratum.

Both in the natural and artificial nests of *C. comalensis* and *minutus* the brood was carefully kept to one side of the damp fungus garden, which would certainly be a very unwholesome and inappropriate nursery compared with the flocculent gardens of other Attii. The larvæ of *comalensis* were fed by the workers with small pieces of the bromatia. I have seen a few virgin females in the nests of this variety as early as May 10, but these and the males were not found in numbers till June 10 to 21. In the more southern countries, such as Culebra and Porto Rico, the winged phases appear as early as March and April. They "feign death" like the workers, but the males less readily than the females.

9.   Atta (Mycocepurus) smithi *Forel.*

This species, originally described from the island of St. Vincent, seems to be widely distributed through the West Indies and Mexico, but I have seen it only in Porto Rico, where it is represented by the variety *borinquenen-*

sis. Owing to its retiring habits and small size, it is very easily overlooked. A few isolated nests were found in the open fields and among the cafetals and platanals along the turnpike which winds through the picturesque mountains between Arecibo and Ponce. These nests and one found in the curiously eroded country about Vega Baja between San Juan and Arecibo, were small, obscure craters less than 8 cm. in diameter, made of earth of a different color from that of the surrounding surface and therefore brought up from some little depth. I made several attempts at excavation but was never able to find the fungus gardens. Finally I discovered a nest in moist red clay under a stone on the shady slope of Mount Morales near Utuado at an altitude of about 400 m. The ants, about 30 in number, had constructed a small tubular entrance at the edge of the stone and had excavated a tenuous gallery about 5 mm. in diameter for a distance of several cm. along the surface covered by the stone to a small irregular chamber. In this I found the fungus garden which consisted of a mass, hardly more than 2 c. cm. in volume, of caterpillar droppings, studded with bromatia which differed from those of *Cyphomyrmex rimosus* only in the somewhat greater volume of their component cells (Pl. LIII, Fig. 44). This difference is, however, probably of little importance, as the material from which the figure was drawn was more recently preserved than that represented in Pl. LIII, Fig. 43. As *C. minutus* and *Mycocepurus borinquenensis* occur in the same localities it is quite possible that both ants may cultivate the same species of fungus.

These observations though very meagre, are nevertheless sufficient to prove that in its habits *Mycocepurus* is much more closely related to *Cyphomyrmex* than to any of the subgenera of *Atta*. It would be permissible therefore to regard *Mycocepurus* as an independent genus.

10. **Myrmicocrypta brittoni** sp. nov.

My brief glimpse of the habits of this Porto Rican ant would be hardly worth recording, were it not that no observations have been published on the habits of the remarkable genus *Myrmicocrypta*. *M. brittoni* was seen only at Santurce, a suburb of San Juan, while I was accompanying Professor N. L. Britton on a botanical excursion. The ants were nesting in the sea-beach just above high-water mark and over a narrow strip of the adjacent shore in a large grove of cocoanut palms. The black workers stood out in strong contrast with the white sand over which they were moving in the bright sunlight. The nests, which were very numerous and often only a few meters apart, resembled those of *Trachymyrmex turrifex* as they were in the form of flat, circular craters, 8–10 cm. in diameter, very shallow in the middle and with the vertical entrance gallery terminating on a small turret about a centimeter high.   Under the palms the sand of the craters was often of a deep red color, unlike that of the surrounding surface, so that the galleries must have been rather deep.   Unfortunately my stay in this locality was so brief that I could not examine the nests at my leisure.   Although I subsequently collected in many localities on the island, I never again encountered *M. brittoni.*   Santurce is, however, easily accessible from San Juan, and the future observer will have no difficulty in finding the nests and of learning much more concerning the habits of this interesting ant.

PART IV.   THE ATTII AND THE OTHER FUNGUS-GROWING INSECTS.

Many insects, especially of the orders Coleoptera and Diptera, either in the larval or imaginal stages, are known to feed on fungi, but the ability to cultivate or to control the growth of these food plants is, so far as known, restricted to certain termites, Scolytid beetles and ants.   The taxonomic relationships of these three groups to one another are so remote that we are compelled to regard this control as the result of convergent development. In other words, the fungus-growing habit must have arisen independently on three separate occasions in the phyletic history of the Insecta.   In order to secure a broader comparative basis for a discussion of the fungus-growing habits of the Attii it will be necessary to summarize our knowledge of the similar habits in the termites and ambrosia beetles.

1.   *The Fungus-growing Termites.*

Several observers have undoubtedly seen and described the fungus gardens of termites without being aware of the full significance of their observations.   As these gardens are perforated sponge-like masses filled with the insects and their brood and lying on the floors of subterranean chambers, they have often been regarded as the true nests of the termites. The earliest author to call attention to these structures seems to have been König (1779).   After describing the vaulted, smooth-walled earthen chambers of *Termes fatalis* at Tanjore, he mentions the gardens full of holes and lying on the floors as being "covered with little knots on their outer and inner surfaces, like chagrin skin.   This texture is most clearly seen at their margins near the openings and entrances.   Under a magnifying glass they appear fibrous or woolly."   In the light of our present knowledge it is evident that this fibrous or woolly appearance was caused by the fungus mycelium.

Smeathman (1781) was the first to recognize the growth covering the garden as being that of a fungus, although he was not aware that it bore any important relation to the insects.   In his interesting account of the African *Termes bellicosus* he refers to the gardens as "nurseries."   "There is one remarkable circumstance attending the nurseries.   They are always slightly overgrown with mould, and plentifully sprinkled with small white globules about the size of a small pin's head.   These, at first, Mr. S. took to be the eggs; but on bringing them to the microscope, they evidently appeared to be a species of mushroom, in shape like our eatable mushroom in the young state in which it is pickled.   They appear, when whole, white like snow a little thawed and then frozen again, and when bruised seem composed of an infinite number of pellucid particles, approaching to oval forms and difficult to separate; the mouldiness seems likewise to be the same kind of substance.   The nurseries are inclosed in chambers of clay, like those which contain the provisions, but much larger.   In the early state of the nest they are not larger than a hazel-nut, but in great hills are often as large as a child's head of a year old."   I reproduce in Plate LIII, Figs. 55 and 56, Smeathman's figures of a "nursery," and of three of the "mushrooms" enlarged, as these are the earliest known illustrations of the fungus garden of any insect.

Hagen (1860), in his well-known monograph of the Termitidæ, quotes a communication which he received from Nietner of Ceylon on a species referred to *Termes fatalis*.   This observer describes the vaulted earthen chambers of the nest and the fungus gardens which they contained.   The latter "are hemispherical or broadly conical, flat or concave at the base. They are nowhere attached, but stand out freely in the chambers, from which they may be removed without injury.   They consist of a soft bread-like mass of gnawed wood; are brown in color and when broken open golden gray.   These nests are always found to be full of minute microscopic fungi, the finest and most beautiful imaginable.   The corpuscles, as large as a fine pin's head and composed of small beads, grow in clusters on a net-work of roots and young brood; all resembling crystals of ice or silver."   Nietner "does not believe that this fungus bears any other relation to the termites than that the substance of the nest conduces to its growth.   The bread-like nests, threaded with fungi, consist of small galleries and cells which often contain so many eggs and young that the whole appears to form one living mass."

Although, as shown by these citations, the termite gardens were known long before those of the ants, their true significance was not understood till after the publication of Mœller's work (1893) on the South American Attii. Holtermann in 1899 made the first careful study of the gardens of *Termes taprobanes* and *fatalis* in India and the Malay Archipelago (Singapore, Java and Borneo.)   He says: "These animals build their nests in the ground; once only did I find them nesting in a log.   Notwithstanding their clandestine mode of life, I have been able to investigate hundreds and hundreds of their singular habitations, for I was able to find them easily by means of a species of *Agaricus* which was always rooted in a termite nest.   It was only necessary to follow the stem of the pileus into the earth, although in some cases I had to dig to a depth of a meter."   Like Nietner, Holtermann refers to the fungus gardens as "nests."   These varied from the size of a walnut to that of a man's head and were of a sponge-like structure, full of holes and galleries containing termite eggs, larvæ and nymphs.   The gardens were found resting on the floor of the earthen chambers and were separated from the walls by a space as broad as one's finger.   They consisted of finely comminuted vegetable substances (portions of dead leaves and stems) that had passed through the bodies of the termites.   Under the microscope "the surfaces of the galleries were seen to be covered with a white felt-work of mycelium.   Usually the hyphæ were loosely united but sometimes they were combined in strands.   The individual hyphæ were richly septate but showed no 'Schnallenbildung' at the septa."   Even with the unaided eye Holtermann could detect aërial hyphæ projecting from the general felt-work of the mycelium.   "The terminal and often the penultimate cells of these hyphæ were filled with strongly refractive, hyaline protoplasm, whereas the remaining cells contained remarkably little plasma.   The terminal cells were often swollen and club-shaped.   Sometimes the tip even became spherical but only in its upper portion.   In exceptional cases the hyphæ anastomosed, most frequently through confluence of the terminal cells."   This mycelium ramified through the whole substratum which it perhaps served to bind together.   The swollen tips of the hyphæ were often aggregated to form bromatia like those of *Atta*, but Holtermann failed to find them in all termite colonies, and believes that they may occur only in the gardens of certain species.   In addition to these structures he describes others of a more interesting character, namely, small spherical bodies distributed everywhere on the mycelial net-work.   They were white, varied from .25–2 mm. in diameter and were usually attached by a peduncle .5–1 mm. in length.   The minute structure of these spherules which were not abundant in the interior of the garden, is described as follows: "The peduncle consisting of nearly parallel hyphæ becomes wider below and loses itself in the substratum; otherwise it is of uniform thickness and the head is sharply marked off from its end.   The rudiment of the head appears as a distinct thickening at the tip of the stem and as soon as the head is established the stem ceases to grow.   In every chamber are found all the transitions from completed heads to their earliest development in the form of a rich branching at the tip of the bundle of hyphæ forming the stem. The otherwise parallel filaments ramify more and more, till the head is formed. It should be noted that the ends of the filaments do not become thinner while branching but always retain the thickness of the general mycelium. The outer cells grow less rapidly than the others and after a time become passive, thus forming an envelope which later appears as a kind of peridium. The limits of the envelope subsequently become more distinct through the gradual drying up of the outer cells. The inner cells, on the contrary, actively proliferate. The head continues to enlarge owing to the numerous ramifications of the hyphæ, till it has become a sac-like apical thickening. With this increase in size its spherical form changes to an oval. Some time before it attains its complete development, a rapid formation of oïdia takes place in its interior, as the hyphæ break up into very short oval cells. Only here and there a few of the main filaments remain intact, but the lateral branches and greater portion of the hyphæ everywhere break up into short rows of oïdia." These oïdia are 8–25 μ long and 6–10 μ broad and have one or two vacuoles in their protoplasm. So complete is this resolution of the hyphæ of the head into oïdia that a slight pressure on the cover glass causes the dry peridium to burst and thousands of oïdia to escape. Holtermann found that the oïdia are eaten by the termites, but he expressly states that these insects also feed on dead leaves, stems, etc. When the insects are removed from the garden, the cavities of the latter become stuffed with masses of aërial hyphæ, the ripe oïdial heads wither up and alien fungi may make their appearance. Holtermann does not believe that the termites are instrumental in preventing these changes under normal conditions since they occur even when termites are present, if the garden is exposed to the light. The normal condition of the gardens may be due to their confinement in dark subterranean chambers, where the spores of alien fungi are unable to germinate. Holtermann is also of the opinion that the above described fungus represents a form of the mushroom which he found growing out of the nests and calls *Agaricus rajap*. This mushroom has an umber-brown pileus and long gray stem. Its spores are rose-red. He succeeded in growing these spores in a culture liquid, but no oïdial heads were produced although the hyphæ sometimes bore club-shaped swellings. Oïdia from the termite gardens were also sown and slowly produced hyphæ with swollen ends and indistinguishable from those grown from the *Agaricus* spores. This is not, however, conclusive proof of the identity of the two fungi, although it seems to be regarded as such by Holtermann.

Karawaiew (1901) has published in Russian an account of this same fungus which he observed at Buitenzorg, Java. His article is accompanied by some excellent photogravures of the fungus gardens. In Plate LIII, Fig. 57, I have reproduced a portion of one of his figures showing the small oïdial heads apparently of the natural size.

Knuth (1899) observed the fungus gardens of a couple of unidentified species of *Termes* at Buitenzorg, but his description is very meager.

Mme. Errington de la Croix (1900) has published some notes on the Malaccan *Termes carbonarius* which show that the nests of this species contain fungus gardens, although they were not recognized as such. She merely states that they were " formed (perhaps?) by agglomerated eggs in a nutritive substance."

Haviland (1902) figures the nest and gardens of *Termes malayanus* and mentions a number of species of this genus from Africa and southern Asia as fungus growers. These comprise the species of the *bellicosus* group (*T. bellicosus, dives, fatalis, gilvus, azarelli, carbonarius, malaccensis, malayanus, natalensis*), of the *vulgaris* group (*T. vulgaris, angustatus, capensis, taprobanes, badius, latericius*), and of the *incertus* group (*T. incertus* and *pallidus*). Among these are the largest forms of the genus. He states that neoteinic forms, that is, fertile males and females which never develop wings, are not known to occur among fungus-growing termites. The soldiers of some of the species are aggressive and able to make sounds, thus recalling the behavior of the *Atta* soldiers. He says "In the section of the fungus-growers to which *T. bellicosus* belongs the workers run away to their subterranean passages when the nest is being opened, whilst the soldiers stay to defend the nest; generally the smaller soldiers are more active than the larger, for they run about whilst the larger occupy the crevices of the nest and the cavities of the fungus beds, where they wait and bite at anything which comes within reach. The soldiers of this group can generally produce the rattling sound. In this accomplishment, *T. carbonarius* has reached the highest stage of development for the soldiers can hammer in rhythmic unison. At first a few begin irregularly, then they get into time, and the others take it up. Every soldier in the exposed portion of the nest stands up and hammers with its head; the blow is given thrice in very quick succession, and then there is an interval of two seconds. The noise they produce reminded me of wavelets lapping on a shore. This trick of hammering is seen in only a few species; it is clearly a modification of the shaking movements so often seen in workers."

Sjöstedt (1896, 1900, 1903, 1904) has added a number of species to the list of fungus-growing termites from Africa. Such are, for example, *Termes lilljeborgi* and the allied *goliath, gabonensis, nobilis, amplus, gratus* and *vitrialatus*. According to his latest paper (1904) *T. transvaalensis* is also to be included in this series of forms. In his monograph on the African termites (1900) he figures the gardens of *Eutermes heterodon* and describes them as follows: "May 30, 1891, while digging in a hill-slope near the factory N'dian just beside the water fall of the N'dian River a considerable number of the fungus gardens of this species were unearthed. They were as large as walnuts or somewhat smaller and of a light brownish yellow color. They were scattered about in the earth, some a few inches below the surface, others somewhat deeper. The earth between them was perforated with a net-work of galleries, which connected the different beds with one another. Each of the latter was lying free in a cavity so that the termites could move about over it without obstruction. Only here and there were they attached to the adjacent earthen wall. The nest or fungus garden itself is rather fragile and made up of morel-like, folded, and rounded disks separated by a labyrinth of long ventricose or more rarely rounded cavities. The surface is lumpy and shows that the whole consists of spherical particles. The cavities are filled with milkwhite larvæ, workers, and soldiers, the two latter with yellowish brown heads." Sjöstedt's figures of the gardens of *E. heterodon* are reproduced in Plate LIII, Fgs. 60 and 61.

In 1904 Trägårdh published an interesting account of three fungus-growing termites from the Sudan (*T. natalensis, vulgaris* and *trægardhi*). The first builds large conical earthen mounds .8–2.1 m. in height and 1.4 –5.5 m. in diameter at the base. There are no openings on the surface of these mounds, but within they have a number of large chambers, of which only the peripheral ones contain fungus gardens. These are like sponges and conform in shape to the earthen cavities on the floors of which they lie. They are perforated with galleries and consist exclusively of finely comminuted vegetable substances that have been voided and welded together by the insects, for under the microscope they are seen to be made up of pellets that have been flattened into lenticular forms. The fungus growth is described as follows: "Under the microscope the surface of the substratum is seen to be covered with a white felt-work of mycelium and under still higher magnification small hyphæ may be detected. These are aggregated here and there to form small round plates as much as 1 mm. in diameter and consisting of dense branched hyphæ. These apparently correspond to the structures mentioned and described by Holtermann, but differ from these, so far as I have been able to observe, in not having the tips of the hyphæ swollen. Here and there on the inner walls, usually not in any great abundance, but more sporadic, at least in the gardens I have examined, there are small round bodies, which may be as much as 2.5 mm. in diameter. They are of a brilliant white color and are unlike those mentioned by Holtermann in always lacking a peduncle. These spherules are of rather solid consistency and have an external tougher envelope, the whole forming a compact mass of very much branched and contorted hyphæ. The formation of the oïdia, or process whereby, according to Holtermann, the hyphæ in the interior of the spherules breaks up almost completely into very short oval cells, is by no means so complete in our species. To be sure, the hyphæ are constricted in the interior so that they appear as rows of short oval cells, completely filled with protoplasm, but these cells even in the largest spherules, which have reached their full development, remain attached to one another so that when a thin section is pressed under the cover glass, only a few of the cells escape. In the spherules described by Holtermann, on the contrary, slight pressure on the cover-glass sets free thousands of oïdia."

The mounds of *T. vulgaris* (= *affinis* Trägårdh) are as large as those of *natalensis* (1.4 m. high and 5.5 m. in diameter at the base), but the structure and arrangement of the chambers is very different. They are separated by thick walls and communicate with one another by very tenuous galleries. Each chamber has a flat floor with a peripheral groove and an arched roof. The gardens, which are shaped like inverted dishes and are not confined to the smaller peripheral chambers, are often concave beneath, with a ridge around their border fitting into the circular groove in the floor of the chamber. The substratum consists of the same materials as in *natalensis* and is perforated with numerous transverse galleries. Concerning the fungus Trägårdh says: "The spherules are much smaller than in *natalensis*, are like these nonpedunculate, and occur in great numbers on the walls and especially on the roofs of the cavities and galleries in the peripheral portions of the gardens. These portions are also stuffed with larvæ and nymphs. The spherules are unlike those of *T. natalensis* in structure, since as shown in Figs. 2 & 3 Pl. III [reproduced in the present paper as Figs. 58 & 59, Pl. LIII], the cells in the outer layer of the spherules are larger than those in the interior. Both the inner rows of cells, which ramify dichotomously, and the outer ones, are in part empty, in part filled with finely granular protoplasm." Although Trägårdh found fungus-gardens in the nests of *T. trægardhi* (= *incertus* Trägh.) which seems to live as an inquiline in the nests of *T. bellicosus, natalensis* and *vulgaris*, he believes that these had been stolen from the host termites and that *trægardhi* does not itself grow fungi.

Doflein (1905, 1906) has contributed more recent observations on the gardens of termites. He studied colonies of *T. obscuriceps* in Ceylon. The mounds of this species are about 2 m. high and terminate above in one or more huge tubular, chimney-like orifices which open into the galleries and chambers in the interior of the nest. The chambers are about as large as a cocoa-nut or smaller, with smooth walls and excavated to a depth of 1½ m. below the surface. The gardens, which consist of comminuted wood that has passed through the bodies of the insects, are dish-shaped, and there may be several piled one on top of the other in a single chamber.   They are perforated with galleries filled with the termites and their larvæ.   "On taking one of these brown cakes in the hand, one can see with the unaided eyes that its whole surface is covered with a fine bloom of fungus mycelium. When broken open the interior of the galleries is found to be covered with peculiar white spherules about as large as a pin-head (1–2 mm. in diam.)." Doflein's description of the minute structure of these spherules is less explicit than that of Holtermann and Trägårdh, but he actually saw the termites swallow these bodies when they were presented on the point of a sterilized needle.   They were eaten by the larval workers and soldiers and by the adult kings and queens, but the adult workers and soldiers would not take them.   The intestines of the latter contained only comminuted wood in which no fungus elements could be found.   Doflein, is, therefore, of the opinion "that in this species the larvæ are fed with a concentrated and easily assimilated food in the form of mycelial spherules, and that these constitute the permanent food of the sexual forms, whereas the larvæ of the workers and soldiers are not fed with these after reaching a certain age but with other substances [dead wood] instead.   This suggests the further inference that this food may play an important role in the differentiation of the castes of *Termes obscuriceps* Wasmann."

Doflein found that when the fungus garden of this insect is placed in the light under a bell-jar to protect it from evaporation "the termite fungus can easily be induced to fructify, a peculiarity in which it differs from the fungus cultivated by the South American leaf-cutting ants.   In the course of a few days numerous long, club-shaped fruiting organs grow up out of the dense mass of hyphæ, which has developed in the meantime.   As time goes on these club-shaped bodies develop pilei, which, as Mr. Green of Pera-denyia informs me, are now known to be those of an *Agaricus*, a fact which is also indicated by my own observations.   While the fungus is growing up freely in this manner, one is surprised to find alien fungi gradually making their appearance in the garden, and other objects in the neighborhood taking on the usual mouldiness.   The tendency of the termite fungus to grow as a pure culture must therefore be very great.   This is the case even when very few termites are present.   Hence the purity of the culture cannot be ascribed to a ceaseless weeding process carried on by the termite workers, like that assumed by Mœller in the case of the South American *Attæ*."

When the garden is left under the bell-jar the under surface of the latter soon becomes wet, showing that the fungus gives off a great deal of water. In a day or two the termites become suffocated, although masses of these insects hermetically sealed between pairs of watch glasses manage to live in perfect condition. On raising the bell-jar a peculiar odor is noticeable, which Doflein believes to be a gas fatal to the insects. In the wild nests this gas must be carried off by the chimneys which thus act as ventilating shafts.

All of the foregoing observations relate to Old World Termites. One is naturally led to inquire whether any of the American species raise mushrooms. Haviland was of the opinion that certain of the South American forms such as *T. dirus* are "almost certainly fungus growers." The only observations I have found on the habits of this species are contained in Silvestri's work (1903). He says: "I have seen in the galleries (Fig. 298) pieces of grass 10 mm. long, of leaves 6–10 mm. long and twigs 30 mm. long and 2 mm. in diameter. I have found such materials accumulated in small quantities at various points in the galleries, but I believe that they are not utilized in this form but are brought together in some more subterranean portion of the nest for the development of a fungus on the mycelium of which the termites feed." He found similar vegetable fragments in the nests of *T. grandis* and *molestus*. Of the latter species he says: "I was unable to reach the center of the nest, but I succeeded in finding small masses of grass with the mycelium already developed." From these, which he figures, he concludes that the species grows fungi. But these observations are by no means conclusive as is evident from a comparison with the above cited observations on the Old World species. These do not raise fungi on pieces of dead leaves, twigs, etc., but on finely comminuted particles voided from the alimentary canal and built up in the form of a sponge. Moreover the temporary stores of leaves, etc. which are brought into the nests as food may easily mould when left in the moist galleries. We may conclude therefore that there is really nothing in Silvestri's observations to prove that any of the South American termites eat and grow fungi.

The most important study of the fungus-growing termites has been recently contributed by Petch (1906). Unfortunately I could not consult this work till after the present article had gone to press, so that I am unable to review it at length. Petch carefully investigated the habits and fungus gardens of the Ceylonese *Termes obscuriceps* Wasm. and *T. redemanni* Wasm. In several particulars his account differs from those of Holtermann and Doflein. I quote from the summary of his beautifully illustrated paper the passages relating to the fungi for the purpose of showing how complex and difficult are the problems with which the mycologist is confronted in any critical study of the fungus-growing insects. After describing the sponge-like combs in the chambers of the nest, he says:[1]

"The mycelium on the comb bears small white, stalked or almost sessile

---

[1] In the quotation I have omitted the numerals belonging to the paragraphs and have run the latter together.

'spheres.' These consist of branching hyphæ bearing either spherical or oval cells. The spherical cells do not germinate. The oval cells germinate readily, but it has not been possible to reproduce the 'spheres' from them. When the comb is old an agaric grows from it. This agaric appears in two forms, one of which has been assigned by various mycologists to *Lentinus, Collybia, Pluteus, Pholiota* and *Flammula,* and the other to *Armillaria.* It develops in a cartilaginous, almost gelatinous, universal veil and is a modified *Volvaria.* Sclerenchymatous cells occur at the base of the agaric stalk and in aborted agarics. It has not been possible to germinate the spores of the agaric or to grow the sphere-producing mycelium from its tissues. When the comb is enclosed in a bell jar, *Xylaria* stromata are produced. Sclerotia may also be formed: the same stromata grow from these. This *Xylaria* is probably *X. nigripes.* The shape of the stroma and conidiophore depend on the age of, and amount of moisture in, the comb. When sown on agar the spores of these reproduce the *Xylaria* stromata. These stromata occur most abundantly in combs which have produced an agaric. After continued rain *Xylaria nigripes* grows from deserted termite nests. Other fungi which grow on combs removed from the nest include *Mucor, Thamnidium, Cephalosporium, Peziza.* As these are not found in the nest though some of them are capable of development under ground, it is probable that the termites 'weed out' foreign fungi from the cultivation of the comb. The comb material is probably sterilized by its passage through the alimentary canal. That the 'spheres' form the food of the termites is probable, as in the case of the leaf-cutting ants: neither case can be considered definitely proved. *Termes redemanni* and *T. obscuriceps* undoubtedly prefer fungi, or wood which has been attacked by fungi. Whether a difference in food causes the differentiation of termites into workers, soldiers, and sexed insects, is not decided. A Ceylon agaric, *Entoloma microcarpum,* possesses a mycelium composed of spheres of swollen cells: the details of these spheres resemble the parts of the termite spheres, but are not so highly developed. It is most probable that the 'spheres' in the termite comb and the 'Kohlrabihäufchen' of the leaf-cutting ants investigated by Mœller are parts of a normal mycelium, and that their shape is modified by the insects only in a very slight degree, if at all. The available evidence appears to show that the 'spheres' are part of the mycelium of the *Volvaria,* but it has not been possible to connect these forms experimentally." A review covering some other features of Petch's work has just been published by Harris in the American Naturalist (1907).

The foregoing accounts from several observers show that the fungus-growing termites differ from the Attiine ants in several important particulars. In the first place the termites use their own excrement as a substratum, moulding it into the form of a sponge containing numerous habitable chambers and galleries. This substance is, of course, much harder and more compact than the comminuted leaves, etc., employed by the Attii.   Second, the fungus grown on this substratum forms bromatia (the spherules or oïdial heads) of a very different type from those found in the gardens of the Attii. And third, the termites that are in the habit of growing fungi are not exclusively mycetophagous like the Attii, but subsist also and probably very largely on dead wood, twigs and leaves. If it be true as Holtermann and Doflein believe, that the termites are not instrumental in maintaining the purity of the fungus culture, we should have another striking difference, but it is quite conceivable that both in the termites and the ants some effluviæ emanating from the myriads of insect bodies may be responsible not only for the suppression of alien fungi but also for the aberrant growth of the food-plant.

I have already called attention to the fact that Holtermann cannot be said to have demonstrated that the *Agaricus rajap* is the fruiting form of the fungus which grows in the gardens as a mycelium with oïdial spherules. And Doflein's and Petch's observations are open to similar doubts.   Not only is there no satisfactory proof that the termite fungus is a basidiomycete, but the same is true also of Mœller's statement that the South American *Attæ* cultivate the mycelium of a fungus (*Rozites gongylophora*) belonging to the same group. A careful perusal of Mœller's observations shows an important lacuna at this point. That his *Attæ* ate portions of the pileus and stem of the *Rozites* does not prove that it is the fruiting form belonging to the fungus they habitually cultivate and eat. Nor is Mœller on much surer ground when he assumes that the mycelia cultivated by different genera of Attii belong to different species of fungi, for it is very probable that the ants of one species would avoid fungus taken from the nest of another on account of the alien nest-aura.   Certainly, to the human olfactories the fungus gardens of *Atta texana* have a very striking odor which is altogether lacking in the gardens of *Trachymyrmex*, and it would be strange if these differences did not affect the appetites of such sensitive insects as the ants.   In my opinion, it is not improbable that the fungi cultivated both by the termites and ants may be more closely related to the moulds (Ascomycetes) than to the mushrooms (Basidiomycetes). Mœller does in fact, call attention to certain ascomycete peculiarities in the mycelium cultivated by *Acromyrmex discigera*. This is a matter, however, to be settled by the mycologist, and I merely call attention to it in this connection, because Mœller's somewhat guarded statements have assumed an unduly positive form in the writings of subsequent reviewers of his work.

2. *The Ambrosia Beetles.*

The beetles of the family Scolytidæ may be divided into two groups exhibiting very different ethological peculiarities: the bark-borers, which excavate and inhabit tubular galleries between the bark and the splint and eat the substance of the tree, and the wood-borers, or ambrosia beetles, which extend their galleries into the wood and subsist on delicate fungi growing on their walls.   All Scolytidæ are of small size and dark color, with cylindrical bodies and short legs adapted to the shape and size of their galleries (Pl. LII, Figs. 62 and 63), but the mouth-parts differ in the two groups; the bark-beetles having strong maxillæ armed with 12–20 spine-like teeth in adaptation to their hard food, whereas the fungus-eating wood-borers have weak maxillæ with 30–40 flexuous bristles.   Unlike the Attii and fungus-growing termites, the wood-borers are not confined to the tropics or to a single hemisphere, but are cosmopolitan in their distribution and well represented even in the north temperate zone.   The species have been assigned to a number of genera (*Platypus, Gnathotrichus, Trypodendron, Xyleborus, Xyloterus, Corthylus* and *Pterocyclon* [*Monarthrum*]).   As these insects are very destructive to wood, they are well known to economic entomologists, who have described their habits in journals or text-books devoted to forestry.   The remarkable habits have therefore been little noticed by entomologists interested in general biological questions.

There has been considerable difference of opinion in regard to the feeding habits of the ambrosia beetles since the time of Schmidberger (1836) who believed that *Xyleborus dispar* Fabr. fed on the sap exuding into its burrows from the surrounding wood.   The mother beetle was supposed to mould this sap into a coagulated, albuminoid mass and to feed it to her young.   This substance Schmidberger called "ambrosia."   Various conjectures concerning its nature were expressed by Ratzeburg (1839–1844), Altum (1872–1875), and Eichhoff (1881).   In 1844 Hartig discovered a fungus in the galleries of *Xyleborus dispar* and described it as *Monilia candida.* Several years later (1872*a*, 1872*b*) he described similar conditions in *Xyloterus lineatus* Oliv., which lives only in conifers, and *X. domesticus* L., which is confined to deciduous trees.   In 1895 Goethe published a good description and figure of the fungus of *X. dispar*.   At about this time Hubbard took up the study of the North American ambrosia beetles and published most interesting accounts of their habits (1897*a*, 1897*b*).   Hopkins, too, who has given special attention to our Scolytidæ, has published a number of valuable observations (1898–1904*b*), and Hedgcock (1906) has made some important observations on the fungi.   In the following paragraphs I shall confine myself to an account of the investigations of these three authors.

The ambrosia beetles resemble the ants and termites and differ from other Coleoptera in living in societies and in caring for and feeding their larvæ. The arrangement of the galleries, which have walls stained dark by the fungus, differs in different species. Those of *Xyleborus celsus* Eichh., living in the hickory, are shown in Pl. LII, Fig. 64, taken from Hopkins (1904). The galleries ramify into the sapwood from a single entrance gallery that opens on the bark. These perforations do not necessarily kill the tree, but they spoil the wood for many commercial purposes. When made in young growing trees they may be overgrown by succeeding layers of wood. Hopkins (1903) has given an interesting account of this condition in trees infested with the Columbian timber-beetle (*Corthylus columbianus* Hopkins). This beetle which is responsible for losses to the lumber interests of North America "amounting to millions of dollars, attacks the sap-wood of the young, living, healthy tree, in which the adults excavate their brood galleries and deposit their eggs. These hatch and develop into beetles and emerge within one year. The next year the operation is repeated in another place in the same tree, and so on for hundreds of years, or as long as the tree lives, so that the galleries excavated in different years and periods occupy their respective positions in the heartwood and sapwood of the full-grown and old tree. Nearly all the damage by this insect, as affecting the best part of the trees, was done 50, 100, 200 or in some cases, as noted in an old tulip tree, over 400 years ago. The age of each gallery observed in the end of the log is easily determined by counting the number of annual layers of wood between the old healed-over entrance to the galleries and the bark. Within recent years, examples of the species which do this work have been exceedingly scarce; consequently but little evidence of its work can now be found in the sapwood and outer heartwood of living trees. Therefore there is no remedy for the old work and probably no need of trying to combat an insect which is apparently becoming extinct."

Hubbard's general account (1897*a*) of the fungus growing habits of the ambrosia beetles is worth quoting *in extenso*, as it is one of the most important of recent contributions to the study of insect ethology: "A small fragment of ambrosia taken from the gallery of any species of these timber beetles, if placed on a glass slide, with a drop of water or glycerine and examined with an objective of moderate power, is plainly seen to be a fungus. It will be found, however, that the different kinds of ambrosia fungi are connected with certain species of the beetles irrespective of the sort of timber in which the galleries are constructed. So far as we yet know the food of each species of ambrosia beetles is limited to a certain kind of ambrosia, and only the most closely related species have the same food fungus.

"Two principal types exist among the varied forms of these minute fungi: (1) Those with erect stems, having at the termination of the stems, or their branches swollen cells (conidia) [Pl. LII, Fig. 65]. (2) Those which form tangled chains of cells resembling the piled-up beads of a broken necklace. The erect or stylate forms are found among those species of the beetles whose larvæ live free in the galleries (*Platypus* and *Xyleborus*). The bead-like or moniliform kinds appear to be peculiar to the species whose larvæ are reared in separate cells or cradles (*Corthylus, Monarthrum*, etc.).

"All the growing parts of the fungus are extremely succulent and tender. The conidia especially are always pellucid, and glisten like drops of dew. When the plant is in active growth, conidia are produced in the greatest abundance, growing sometimes singly, at the end of short straight stems, sometimes in grape-like clusters among interlacing branches. At such periods the fungus appears upon the walls of the galleries like a coating of hoarfrost. The young larvæ nip off these tender tips as calves crop the heads of clover, but the older larvæ and the adult beetles eat the whole structure down to the base, from which it soon springs up afresh, appearing in little white tesselations upon the walls.

"The growth of ambrosia may in fact be compared to asparagus, which remains succulent and edible only when continually cropped, but if allowed to go to seed is no longer useful as food. In like manner the ambrosia fungus must be constantly kept in fresh growth, otherwise it ripens; its cells burst and discharge the protoplasmic granules which they contain in myriads, and the entire plant disappears as if overwhelmed by a ferment.

"Various disturbances of the conditions necessary to its growth are apt to promote the ripening of the fungus, and this is a danger to which every colony of ambrosia beetles is exposed. If through any casualty the natural increase of a populous colony is checked, there results at once an overproduction of the ambrosia. It accumulates, ripens, and discharges its spores, choking the galleries and often suffocating the remaining inhabitants in their own food material. The same results may sometimes be brought about by closing the outlets of the galleries through the bark, or by spraying into them kerosene or some other noxious liquid. The inmates of the colony are thereby thrown into a panic, the beetles rush hither and thither through the galleries, trampling upon and crushing young larvæ and eggs, breaking down the delicate lining of ambrosia on the walls of the brood chambers and puddling it into a kind of a slush, which is pushed along and accumulated in the passage ways, completely stopping them in places. The breaking down of the food fungus follows and in a few days the galleries are filled with a paste-like mass of granules or spores, or with threads of mycelium, in which the living insects are suffocated and destroyed.

"The ambrosia does not make its appearance by accident or at random in the galleries of the beetles. Its origin is entirely under the control of the insect. It is started by the mother beetle upon a carefully packed bed or layer of chips, sometimes near the entrance, in the bark, but generally at the end of a branch gallery in the wood. In some species the ambrosia is grown only in certain brood chambers of peculiar construction. In others it is propagated in beds, near the cradles of the larvæ. The excrement of the larvæ is used in some and probably in all species to form new beds or layers for the propagation of the fungus.

"It is not alone, however, the excreta of the living beetles or their young that is required for the development of ambrosia; there must be present a certain amount of moisture or sap, and the sap in most species must be in a condition of fermentation. Certain ambrosia beetles, as for example the species of *Corthylus*, seem not to need fermentation in the propagation of their fungus; their galleries are constructed in the sap-wood of vigorous plants. The great majority of the species, however, attack the wood of such trees only as are moribund; in which the natural circulation of the sap has ceased, and fermentation has begun. Some of the number are also able to produce their food fungus in wood which is saturated with a vinous or alcoholic ferment, and they attack wine and ale casks, perforating the staves with their galleries and causing serious loss by leakage.

"The precarious conditions under which their food is produced limit the life of a colony of ambrosia eaters in most cases to a single generation.

"Under favorable conditions, and in large tree trunks, colonies may continue their excavations during two or three generations before the failure of the sap or change in its condition puts an end to their existence and forces the adult beetles to seek new quarters.

"When their galleries are disturbed and opened to daylight, the adult beetles generally fall to eating their ambrosia as rapidly as possible. Like other social insects they show their concern at the threatened loss of their most precious possession and try to save it, just as bees, when alarmed, fill themselves with honey.

"As its honey is to the bee, so to the ambrosia-feeding beetle its food fungus is the material the propagation and preservation of which is the chief concern of its life. Its solicitude concerning it is not surprising when one considers the herculean labors which it undergoes in the effort to produce it, the frequent failures, and the difficulties and uncertainties that at all times attend its preservation in the vegetative form, in which alone it can serve the insect as food."

The life-histories of the ambrosia beetles described and copiously illustrated by Hubbard suggest a wide range of habits within the group. The genus *Platypus*, though best represented in the tropics, contains several of the largest and most destructive species in the United States. "They are powerful excavators, generally selecting the trunks of large trees and driving their galleries deep into the heart-wood. They do not attack healthy trees but are attracted only by the fermenting of the sap of dying or very badly injured trees. The death rattle is not more ominous of dissolution in animals than the presence of these beetles in standing timber....The female is frequently accompanied by several males and as they are savage fighters, fierce sexual contests take place, as a result of which the galleries are often strewn with the fragments of the vanquished. The projecting spines at the end of the wing-cases are very effective weapons in these fights. With their aid a beetle attacked in the rear can make a good defense and frequently by a lucky stroke is able to dislocate the outstretched neck of his enemy. The females produce from 100 to 200 elongate-oval pearl-white eggs, which they deposit, in clusters of 10 or 12, loosely in the galleries. The young require five or six weeks for their development. They wander about in the passages and feed in company upon the ambrosia which grows here and there upon the walls....The older larvæ assist in excavating the galleries, but they do not eat or swallow the wood. The larvæ of all ages are surprisingly alert, active and intelligent. They exhibit curiosity equally with the adults, or show evident regard for the eggs and very tender young, which are scattered at random about the passages, and might easily be destroyed by them in their movements. If thrown into a panic the young larvæ scurry away with an undulatory movement of their bodies, but the older larvæ will frequently stop at the nearest intersecting passage and show fight to cover their retreat." The ambrosia of *P. compositus* Say consists of hemispherical conidia growing in clusters on branching stems. The long continued growth of this fungus blackens the walls of the older galleries.

Xyleborus saxeseni Ratzb., instead of producing ramifying galleries, excavates in hardwood trees (oak, hickory, beech, maple) a flat, leaf-shaped brood chamber connected with the surface of the bark by one or a few tubular galleries. The chamber "stands vertically on edge, parallel with the grain of the wood. The space between the walls is not much greater than the thickness of the bodies of the adult beetles. The larvæ of all ages are able to cling to the vertical walls, and to progress over them by an adaptation of the end of the body which aids them in progression. The entire surfaces of the walls in the brood chamber are plastered over with ambrosia fungus. It consists of short erect stems, terminating in spherical conidia. The freshly grown fungus is as colorless as crystal, but it is usually more or less stained with greenish yellow, and sometimes resembles a coating of sublimed sulphur. The brood chamber is packed at times with eggs, larvæ, pupæ and adults in all stages of maturity. The larvæ aid in extending the brood chamber. They swallow the wood which they remove with their jaws, and in passing through their bodies it becomes stained a mustard-yellow color. Great quantities of this excrement are ejected from the openings of the colony, but a portion is retained and plastered upon the walls, where it serves as a bed upon which there springs up a new crop of the food fungus. In populous colonies it is not unusual to find the remains of individuals which have died packed away in a deep recess of the brood chamber and carefully inclosed with a wall of chips." Hubbard found one of these catacombs containing "the multilated bodies of a dozen or more larvæ and immature imagoes, together with the fragments of a predatory beetle, *Colydium lineola* Say." In a short branch gallery of the same chamber he also found the lifeless body of the mother of the colony carefully sealed up by the surviving insects.

In the species of *Pterocyclon, Xyloberus* and *Gnathotrichus* the young are reared in cradles, or short diverticula of the main galleries, and fed by the mother beetles. In species of *Ptercyclon* (*mali* Fitch and *fasciatum* Say) "the sexes are alike, and the males assist the females in forming new colonies. The young are raised in separate pits or cradles which they never leave until they reach the adult stage. The galleries, constructed by the mature female beetles, extend rather deeply into the wood, with their branches mostly in a horizontal plane. The mother beetle deposits her eggs singly in circular pits which she excavates in the gallery in two opposite series, parallel with the grain of the wood. The eggs are loosely packed in the pits with chips and material taken from the fungus bed which she has previously prepared in the vicinity and upon which the ambrosia has begun to grow. The young larvæ, as soon as they hatch out, eat the fungus from these chips and eject the refuse from their cradles. At first they lie curled up in the pit made by the mother, but as they grow larger, with their own jaws they deepen their cradles, until, at full growth, they slightly exceed the length of the larvæ when fully extended. The larvæ swallow the wood which they excavate, but do not digest it. It passes through the intestines unchanged in cellular texture, but cemented by the excrement into pellets and stained a yellowish color. The pellets of excrement are not allowed by the larvæ to accumulate in their cradles, but are frequently ejected by them and are removed and cast out of the mouth of the borings by the mother beetle. A portion of the excrement is evidently utilized to form the fungus bed. The mother beetle is constantly in attendance upon her young during the period of their development, and guards them with jealous care. The mouth of each cradle is closed with a plug of the food fungus, and as fast as this is consumed it is renewed with fresh material. The larvæ from time to time perforate this plug and clean out their cells, pushing out the pellets of excrement through the opening. This débris is promptly removed by the mother and the opening again sealed with ambrosia. The young transform to perfect beetles before leaving their cradles and emerging into the galleries." The ambrosia of *Pterocyclon* "is moniliform and resembles a mass of pearly beads. In its incipient stages a formative stem is seen, which has short joints that become globular conidia and break apart. Short chains of cells, sometimes showing branches, may often be separated from the mass. The base of the fungus mass is stained with a tinge of green, but the stain on the wood is almost black."

In *Xyloterus retusus* Lec., which lives in the broad-toothed aspen (*Populus grandidentata*) of the northern States, and is the largest of our ambrosia beetles, still other peculiarities are observable. "Several pairs of the beetle unite in colonies having a single entrance, but each family occupies its own quarters, consisting of one or two branch galleries. The galleries do not penetrate deeply into the heart-wood. Each female attends her own brood, which are raised in cradles extending upward and downward at right angles to the main passage-way. She feeds the young with a yellowish ambrosia grown in beds in the neighborhood of the cradles. The mouth of each cradle is constantly kept filled with a plug of the food fungus. The ambrosia consists of oval cells which form upright sticks resembling some forms of styliform ambrosia, but they do not branch and are capable of being broken up into beadlike masses without losing their vegetative powers. Although the color of the fungus is yellowish, the galleries are stained intensely black."

The foregoing account of the ambrosia beetles suggests a number of intricate and important problems for future investigation. That these insects have developed unusually advanced social habits for Coleoptera is certain. It is also evident that the fungi which they cultivate are not basidiomycetes but chromatogenic or wood-staining ascomycetes. Hedgcock (1906) who has recently studied these fungi, describes a number of species referable to the genera *Ceratostomella* (wood-bluing), *Graphium, Hormodendron, Hormiscium* (wood blackening and wood-browning), *Penicillium* and *Fusarium* (wood-reddening). Cultures of one of the species (*Graphium ambrosiigerum* Hedgc.) were made from material taken from the burrows of ambrosia beetles in the wood of *Pinus arizonica* Eng. The mycelium was seen to develop stromata with heads, and both primary and secondary conidia, but the author records no observations on the relations of the beetle to the fungus or the modifications produced in the food plant when in the presence of the insect. From some investigations now in progress at the Royal School of Forestry at Tharandt, Saxony, and communicated to me by Professors K. Escherich and F. W. Neger it would seem that in the case of the ambrosia beetle *Trypodendron lineatus* the fungus is found only in the mycelial and conidial stages when the insects are present, but that when these have been removed stromata with globular or flattened heads, similar to those figured by Hedgcock for *Graphium atrovirens* and *ambrosii-gerum*, are produced on the walls of the galleries.

The constant association of certain species of ambrosia beetles with certain species of fungi, irrespective of the kind of wood on which they grow, indicates that the mother beetles must be instrumental in transferring the plant from colony to colony and from tree to tree in some manner analogous to the fungus transfer of the *Atta* queen when establishing her formicary. Hedgcock seems to have found evidence of some such transference of *Ceratostomella* conidia. He says: "These are readily disseminated by the wind and are probably carried by insects which penetrate the wood and bark of trees, like most of the ambrosia and bark beetles. At the stage in which the conidia form a mucilaginous mass, they adhere readily to any insect that may pass over them. In the laboratory a number of species of mites which feed on fungi carried spores on their bodies from colony to colony in an agar plate to a sterile portion of the surface of the medium and started new colonies of the fungus. Bark beetles were placed in a dish with the conidial stage of *Ceratostomella* and after allowing them to remain a short time were transferred to sterile agar plates which were inoculated with spores from the insects. It is probable that some species of insects feed on the conidial stage of *Ceratostomella*, especially one or more species of ambrosia beetles and a number of mites infesting their channels in the wood; but proof is yet lacking on this point. The constant occurrence of this fungus in the channels of a number of wood boring beetles indicates that the conidia or the ascospores must be carried in some manner by these insects."

Interesting as are the observations on the fungicolous ants, termites and beetles collated in the preceding pages, we must admit that they are still fragmentary and leave many fundamental questions unanswered. It will be seen that our knowledge of the fungi cultivated by all three of these insect groups is very unsatisfactory and that many more investigations must be undertaken before we shall be able to determine the precise taxonomic affinities of the plants and to estimate the extent of the modifications induced in their growth by the symbiotic insects. Equally fragmentary is our knowledge of the phylogenetic origin and development of the fungus-growing habit. Indeed, this problem in the termites and ambrosia beetles has scarcely been recognized a yet. The views that have been entertained in regard to the phylogeny of the Attii and their habits are perhaps, of sufficient interest to command attention till further observations are forthcoming.

3. *The Phylogeny of the Attii and of the Fungus-growing Habit.*

The Attii belong to a complex of Myrmicine genera once grouped together as Cryptocerides on account of their superficial resemblance to the
ants of the genus *Cryptocerus.*   Forel in 1892 was the first to split up this
artificial group.   He divided the genera into four tribes, the first including
the Attini, the second the Dacetonini, again divisible into three subgroups:
a, Strumigenys, Orectognathus, Epitritus and possibly *Hypopomyrmex;*
b, Daceton and *Acanthognathus,* and *c, Rhopalothrix, Ceratobasis* and
Cataulacus.   To a third tribe he assigned *Meranoplus* and *Calyptomyrmex,*
which were recognized as having affinities with the Tetramorii, and to a
fourth tribe he assigned *Cryptocerus* and *Procryptocerus.*   In 1893 he said:
"Taxonomy has proved to me that the Attini are intimately related to the
Dacetonini (*Strumigenys,* etc.) and has led me to suppose that the Attini
are of secondary derivation.   This is all the more probable, because they are
confined to the American continent, whereas the Dacetonini are distributed
over the whole world, even to New Zealand."

Emery, writing in the same year (1893), expresses himself somewhat
more explicitly.   "If we separate from the *ensemble* of the ancient Cryptocerides, on the one hand *Cryptocerus* and *Procryptocerus* (group Cryptocerini),
on the other hand *Cataulacus* (forming by itself a distinct group), and if
furthermore, *Meranoplus* and *Calyptomyrmex* be attached to *Tetramorium*
and its allies, all that remains of M. Forel's Attini may be divided into two
groups according to the venation of the wings.   In the genera *Atta, Sericomyrmex, Cyphomyrmex, Glyptomyrmex* [*Myrmicocrypta*], *Apterostigma,*
the radial cell is closed and there is no trace of a discal cell nor of a recurrent
nervure, the trunk of the cubital nervure being straight or feebly sinuous.
In the genera *Rhopalothrix, Strumigenys* and *Epitritus* the radial cell is
open; in the female *Rhopalothrix petiolata* Mayr I find a vestige of a recurrent nervure, and in the male *Strumigenys imitator* Mayr the trunk of the
cubital vein is strongly arcuate behind at the base, indicating the point of
insertion of a recurrent nervure that has disappeared.   According to Smith's
figures, *Daceton,* which has a discal cell, belongs to this latter group;
probably the same is true of *Acanthognathus, Ceratobasis* and *Orectognathus,*
whose wings are still unknown.   The former of these two groups, which we
may call the *Attini genuini* is exclusively American, whereas the latter,
which may bear the name Dacetini, is represented in all the zoological regions
except the Ethiopian.   These two groups are, however, very closely allied,
and the fossil genus *Hypopomyrmex,* which undoubtedly approaches the
ancestors of *Strumigenys* very closely, has a discal and a closed radial
cell.   The closed radial cell is an archaic character and is found only in a

few Myrmicine genera, such as *Cryptocerus, Atopomyrmex, Myrmecina, Pheidologeton, Aëromyrma, Carebara, Lophomyrmex* and certain species of *Tetramorium*. In my opinion no great taxonomic importance is to be attached to this character; nevertheless its constant occurrence in the true Attini must be taken into consideration."

In a later paper (1895) Emery groups the genera above mentioned as follows:

Tribe Dacetii: *Daceton, Acanthognathus, Orectognathus, Strumigenys, Epitritus, Rhopalothrix, Ceratobasis*.

Tribe Attii: embracing besides the genera and subgenera enumerated in the introduction to this paper, *Wasmannia* and possibly also *Ochetomyrmex*.

Tribe Cryptocerii: *Procryptocerus* and *Cryptocerus*.

Tribe. Cataulacii: *Cataulacus*.

Emery is apparently of the opinion that the Attii are related to the Tetramorii through such intermediate genera as *Wasmannia* and *Ochetomyrmex*, whereas Forel is inclined to seek their origin among the Dacetonii through such a series of genera as *Cyphomyrmex, Rhopalothrix* and *Strumigenys*. Morphological considerations may be adduced in support of either of these contentions. The question then naturally arises as to whether there are in the Dacetonii or Tetramorii any ethological peculiarities which by further development could lead to the highly specialized fungus-growing habits of the Attii.

Forel (1902) regards *Cyphomyrmex* as the most primitive genus of Attii and believes that some of the species do not raise fungi, whereas the others make very imperfect gardens on insect excrement. These ants would thus be transitional in their habits to the Dacetonii, many of which also live in damp places in rotten wood, where fungi grow in abundance and where there is plenty of insect excrement that might gradually come to be employed as a substratum. In an earlier paper (1893) Forel quotes in support of his view an observation of H. Smith on the West Indian *Strumigenys smithi* Forel, a species which nests in rotten wood. Smith says that "the cavities in which these ants are found are *always* black inside, as if with some fungoid growth." Forel infers from this that some species of *Strumigenys* cultivate fungi. It seems to me, however, that his view evaporates into a mere hypothesis when the facts are more closely scrutinized. In the first place, there is no known species of *Cyphomyrmex*, nor in fact any Attiine ant, which does not cultivate fungi. I have shown in the third part of the present paper that statements to the contrary in regard to *C. rimosus* are false and due to superficial observations. In the second place, there is not a particle of evidence to prove that the Dacetonii cultivate fungi. The species discovered by Smith may have been nesting in the abandoned fungus-stained galleries of ambrosia beetles, or the dark color of the walls may have been due to other causes.   I may say also that in no colonies of the various species of *Strumigenys* which I have found in the United States and West Indies were there any traces of fungi.   These ants live in rather small communities under stones or in rotten wood and feed on insects.   Many of our species live as thief ants, after the manner of *Solenopsis molesta* Say, in the nests of larger ants.   *Rhopalothrix* seems to have similar habits, to judge from some field notes accompanying a colony of an undescribed species taken, with all its larvæ and pupæ, under a stone in Jamaica.

Forel's view, however, contains an interesting suggestion, for the nature of the substratum on which the fungi are grown may be supposed to throw some light on the origin of the habit under discussion.   In all the fungicolous insects there is an unmistakable tendency to employ vegetable substances that have passed through the alimentary tract of insects.   This is the case in all fungus-growing termites, and in the ambrosia beetles.   Among the Attii, as I have shown, this tendency is apparent in nearly all the species that have been closely observed.   Though most pronounced in the lower genera and subgenera (*Cyphomyrmex*, *Apterostigma*, *Mycocepurus*, *Trachymyrmex*), it is not wholly lost even in the leaf-cutting *Attæ*, and the method employed by the *Atta* queens in manuring their incipient fungus-gardens suggests that the food plant may have been originally grown on fecal substances.   It is quite possible, however, that in the Attii this habit is secondary and that it was preceded phylogenetically by culture on some other substance since generally abandoned as less suited to the purpose.   This leads us to a consideration of another view on the origin of the fungus-growing habit.

Von Ihering (1894) advances the following opinion: "We know quite a number of ants, like the species of *Pheidole*, *Pogonomyrmex* and furthermore species of *Aphænogaster* and even of *Lasius*, which carry in grain and seeds to be stored as food.   Such grain carried in while still unripe, would necessarily mould and the ants feeding upon it would eat portions of the fungus.   In doing this they might easily come to prefer the fungi to the seeds.   If *Atta lundi* still garners grass seeds and in even greater than the natural proportion to the grass blades, this can only be regarded as a custom which has survived from a previous cultural stage."   Thus von Ihering would explain the origin of fungus cultivation and the supervention of the leaf-cutting habit.

This view, like Forel's, is, of course, purely hypothetical.   There are, however, a few facts which indicate that the Attii may have developed from grain-storing species allied to the Tetramorii (*Meranoplus* and *Tetramorium*) as Emery has suggested.   That certain harvesting species form nests and have many peculiarities of behavior similar to those of the smaller Attii is shown by Santschi's observations on *Oxyopomyrmex santschii* Forel of the Tunisian deserts. In a letter to Forel, Santschi states that the nests of this ant are "so characteristic that when one has once seen one of them, nothing is easier than to find others. I am surprised to find that they have not attracted the attention of other observers. Especially remarkable is the tiny crater, which has the form of a cone, hardly more than 4–5 cm. in diameter and 2.5–3 cm. high. The circumference of its funnel-shaped top is 3–4 cm. across and its margin is always perfectly circular and entire, except in nests in process of construction, where it is at first semilunar like the very small nests of *Messor arenarius*. At the bottom of the funnel the small entrance is found, 1–2 mm. in diameter, just large enough to permit one of the workers to pass. A single nest has rarely two entrances and two cones. A single perpendicular gallery descends below the surface. A first chamber is found at a depth of 2–3 cm. It is horizontal, attaining a length of 5 cm., a breadth of 1 cm. and a height of 5 cm. In this first chamber the pupæ are kept for the purpose of enjoying the warmth and here I have found a number of workers and winged females. Thence the gallery continues to descend to a depth of 15–20 cm. and finally opens into two or three chambers of the same dimensions as the first. These contain pupæ and an ample provision of very small seeds. This ant is therefore granivorous. I surprised a few of the workers entering the nest with seeds in their mandibles. They go out foraging singly and not in files like *Messor* and other genera. They are very slow in their movements and are very apt to stop motionless at the least alarm. Day or night one or two of the workers may be seen on the outer surface of the crater scarcely moving unless molested, but when disturbed they hurriedly retreat into the nest to spread the alarm. Their habits are rather nocturnal. If a light is brought near the nest when a worker is on the point of leaving it with a grain of sand she hurriedly backs into the entrance and there stops, closing it perfectly with her burden. If the observer remains very quiet, she eventually comes forth and deposits her load on the slope of the crater. There are scarcely more than thirty individuals in a nest."

Although *Oxyopomyrmex* has no close taxonomic relations with the Attii or Tetramorii, but rather with members of the complex genus *Stenamma*, it closely resembles *Trachymyrmex turrifex* and *Mycetosoritis hartmanni* in the small size of its colonies, the slowness of its movements and the structure of its nests. These resemblances are in all probability, due to convergent development. Nevertheless, species with habits like *Oxyopomyrmex* might conceivably become fungicolous by some such substitution of instincts as that suggested by von Ihering. So many assumptions, however, would have to be made in order to account for the delicate and intricate adaptations shown by existing Attii in the cultivation of their fungi, that further speculation seems idle till we are in possession of a greater body of careful observavations.

Less hypothetical and worthier of confidence are the views of Forel and von Ihering concerning phylogenetic development within the narrow confines of the Attiine tribe itself. But here, too, we must proceed with caution. The ants of the genera and subgenera *Cyphomyrmex, Myrmicocrypta, Sericomyrmex, Apterostigma, Mycocepurus* and *Mycetosoritis* on the one hand, are obviously primitive, for they form small colonies and have monomorphic workers and proportionally small males and females. On the other hand, *Atta* s. str. would seem to be the most recent and highly specialized genus of the tribe, because the colonies are very populous, the workers are polymorphic with marked division of labor, and the males and females are very large. Between these two groups, *Trachymyrmex, Acromyrmex* and *Mœllerius* occupy an intermediate position. Mœller and subsequent writers have been inclined to find a parallel development in the instincts, but this is not so clear as the morphological sequence and relations of the various genera and subgenera, for we find *Atta* s. str. and *Acromyrmex* building gardens on the floors of their chambers like *Cyphomyrmex*, whereas *Apterostigma* has highly specialized gardens, suspended and enveloped in a mycelial web not known to occur in any other Attii. Moreover, at least one species of *Cyphomyrmex* (*rimosus*) and a species of *Atta* s. lat. (*Mycocepurus smithi*) cultivate a very different fungus from that known to occur in the nests of any other species; *C. wheeleri* does not, at least as a rule, use caterpillar excrement as a substratum but only small plant slivers; *Mycetosoritis* specializes to the extent of using only the anthers of flowers, and *Sericomyrmex opacus* has a predilection for fruit pulp. All of these species are therefore aberrant in their habits, though belonging to primitive genera. Mœller has certainly overestimated the primitive nature of the treatment bestowed on the fungi in the nests of *Cyphomyrmex* as a group, and although the bromatia of the *Apterostigma* gardens may be of a generalized type, this genus is in many other respects more highly specialized than *Atta* s. str.

Granting the cogency of these considerations, it still remains true that the Attii in general present a series of increasingly specialized forms as we pass from the species of *Cyphomyrmex* through the subgenera *Mycetosoritis, Trachymyrmex, Acromyrmex* and *Mœllerius* to *Atta* s. str. in which we see the culmination of a wonderful progress in adaptation. These insects in the fierce struggle for existence, everywhere apparent in the tropics, have developed a complex of instinctive activities which enables them to draw upon an ever-present, inexhaustible food-supply through utilizing the foliage of plants

as a substratum for the cultivation of edible fungi. No wonder therefore, that, having emancipated themselves from the precarious diet of other
ants, which subsist on insects, the sweet exudations of plants and the excrement of phytophthorous Rhynchota, the Attii have become the dominant
invertebrates of tropical America!

BIBLIOGRAPHY.

a. Fungus-growing Ants.

1899. **André, Ernest.** Les Fourmis Champignonnistes. Extr., *Soc. Grayloise
d' Émul*, Année 1899, pp. 3–12.

1892. **Bates, H. W.** The Naturalist on the River Amazon. Ed. by Clodd. London,
1892. First edit. 1863.

1888. **Belt, Thomas.** The Naturalist in Nicaragua. 2d ed., London, 1888
(1st ed. 1874).

1886. **Brent, C.** Notes on the Œcodomas, or Leaf-cutting Ants of Trinidad.
Amer. Natur., XX, no. 2, 1886, pp. 123–131, 7 figs.

1901. **Bolivar, I.** Un Nuevo Ortóptero Mirmecófilo Attaphila bergi. *Com. Mus.
Nac. Buenos Ayres*, I, 1901, pp. 331–336, 1 fig.

1900. **Branner, J. C.** Ants as Geologic Agents in the Tropics. *Journ. Geol.*,
Chicago, VIII, pp. 151–153, 3 figs.

1860. **Buckley, S. B.** The Cutting Ant of Texas (Œcodoma mexicana Sm.).
Proc. Acad. Nat. Sci. Phila., 1860, p. 233; *Ann. Mag. Nat. Hist.* (3), VI,
1860, pp. 386–389.

1886. **Chatrian, N.** La Fourmi Sauva. *Rev. Scientif.* (3), XXXVIII, 1886,
pp. 371–372.

1653. **Cobo, P. Bernabé.** Historia del Nuevo Mundo. 1653 (published in 1892),
II, pp. 261–266, *passim*.

1906. **Cook, M. T.** Insectos y Enfermedades del Naranjo. *Prim. Informe Anual
de la Estac. Centr. Agronomica de Cuba*, Havana, 1906, pp. 149–172.

1879. **Dewitz, H.** Insectenmisbildung. *Zool. Anz.*, 2 Jahrg., 1879, pp. 134–136,
1 fig.

1900. **Dominique, J.** Fourmis Jardinières. *Bull. Soc. Sci. Nat. Ouest. Nantes*,
X, pp. 163–168, 3 figg.

1889. **Emery, Carlo.** Alleanze Difensive tra Piante e Formiche. *Nuova Antologia*,
XIX (3), Feb. 1889, 16 pp.

1890. **Emery, Carlo.** Voyage de M. E. Simon au Venezuela. Formicides, 1890.

1893. **Emery, Carlo.** Formicides de l'Archipel Malais. *Rev. Suisse de Zool. et
Ann. Mus. d'Hist. Nat. Genève*, I, 1893, pp. 187–229, 1 Pl.

1895. **Emery, Carlo.** Die Gattung Dorylus Fabr. und die systematische Einthei-
lung der Formiciden. *Zool. Jahrb.* Abth. f. Syst. VIII, 1895, pp. 685–778,
4 taf. text-figg.

1906. **Escherich, Karl.** Die Ameise. Schilderung ihrer Lebensweise. Braun-
schweig, Fr. Viehweg u. Sohn, 1906, 232 pp., 68 figg.

1892. **Forel, Auguste.** Attini und Cryptocerini. *Mitth. schweiz. Ent. Ges.*, VIII, Heft 9, 1892, pp. 14, 15 (of extract).

1893. **Forel, Auguste.** Formicides de l'Antille St. Vincent. Récoltées par Mons. H. H. Smith. *Trans. Ent. Soc. London*, Dec. 1893, Pt. IV, pp. 333–418.

1896(a). **Forel, Auguste.** Die Fauna und die Lebensweise der Ameisen im Kolumbischen Urwald und in den Antillen. *Verh. Schweiz. Nat. Ges.*, 1896, pp. 148–150; Extr. *Arch. Sci. Physic. Nat. Genève* (4), II, pp. 616, 617.

1896(b). **Forel, Auguste.** Zur Fauna und Lebensweise der Ameisen im kolumbischen Urwald. *Mitth. Schweiz. Entom. Ges.*, IX, Heft 9, 1896, pp. 401–410.

1896(c). **Forel, Auguste.** Quelques Particularités de l'Habitat des Fourmis de l'Amérique Tropicale. *Ann. Soc. Entom. Belg.*, XL, pp. 167–171.

1897. **Forel, Auguste.** Communication Verbale sur les Mœurs des Fourmis de l'Amérique Tropicale. *Ann. Soc. Entom. Belg.*, XLI, pp. 329–332; Extr. *Feuille Jeun. Nat.* (3), Ann. 23, no. 427, p. 54.

1898. **Forel, Auguste.** La Parabiose chez les Fourmis. *Bull. Soc. Vaud. Sci. Nat.* (4), XXXIV, 1898, pp. 380–384.

1899–1900(a). **Forel, Auguste.** Ebauche sur les Moeurs des Fourmis de l'Amerique du Nord. *Rivista di Sci. Biol.*, no. 3, II, 1900, 13 pp. Also in part in *Ann. Soc. Entom. Belg.*, XLIII, 1899, pp. 438–447. Translation in *Psyche*, IX, 1901, pp. 231–239, 243–245.

1899–1900(b). **Forel, Auguste.** Biologia Centrali-Americana. Hymenoptera III. Formicidæ, 1899–1900, pp. 169, 4 pll.

1901. **Forel, Auguste.** Fourmis Termitophages, Lestobiose, Atta tardigrada, Sousgenres d'Euponera. *Ann. Soc. Entom. Belg.*, XLV, 1901, pp. 389–398.

1902. **Forel, Auguste.** Beispiele phylogenetischer Wirkungen ·und Rückwirkungen bei den Instinkten und dem Körperbau der Ameisen als Belege für die Evolutionslehre und die psychophysische Identitätslehre. *Journ. f. Psychol. u. Neurol.*, I, 1902, pp. 99–110.

1905. **Forel, Auguste.** Einige biologische Beobachtungen des Herrn Prof. Dr. Göldi an brasilianischen Ameisen. *Biol. Centralbl.*, XXV, 1905, pp. 170–181, 7 figg.

1894. **Gibson, R. J. H.** The Mushroom Beds of the South American Ants. *Proc. Liverpool Lit. Soc.*, XLVIII, 1894, pp. 99–105.

1905(a). **Gœldi, E.** Beobachtungen über die erste Anlage einer neuen Kolonie von Atta cephalotes. *C. R. 6me Congr. Internat. Zool. Berne*, 1905, pp. 457, 458.

1905(b). **Gœldi, E.** Myrmecologische Mittheilung das Wachsen des Pilzgartens bei Atta cephalotes betreffend. *Ibid.*, pp. 508–509.

1905. **Huber, Jakob.** Ueber die Koloniengründung bei Atta sexdens. *Biol. Centralbl.*, XXV, pp. 606–619, 625–635, 26 figg.

1882. **von Ihering, H.** Ueber Schichtenbildung durch Ameisen (Atta cephalotes). Briefl. Mitth. aus Mundoro, Rio Grande do Sul, Brasilien, Oct. 1881. *Neues Jahrb. Mineral.*, 1882, I, pp. 156, 157.

1894. **von Ihering, H.** Die Ameisen von Rio Grande do Sul. *Berl. Entom. Zeitschr.*, XXXIX, 1894, pp. 321–446, 1 pl., text figg.

1898. **von Ihering, H.** Die Anlage neuer Colonien und Pilzgärten bei Atta sexdens. *Zool. Anzeig.*, 21 Jahrg., 1898, pp. 238–245, 1 fig.

1900. **Lagerheim, G.** Ueber Lasius fuliginosus (Latr.) und seine Pilzzucht. *Entom. Tidskr.*, Årg. 21, 1900, pp. 17–29.

1901. **Ledebur, A.** Ueber Pilze züchtende Ameisen. *Nerthus*, Jahrg. 3, pp. 411–414, 422–425.

1867. **Lincecum. G.** The Cutting Ant of Texas (Œcodoma Texana). *Proc. Acad. Nat. Sci. Phila.*, 1867, pp. 24–31.

1831. **Lund, A. W.** Lettre sur les Habitudes de quelques Fourmis du Brésil, addressée à M. Audouin. *Ann. Sci. Nat.*, XXIII, 1831, pp. 113–138.

1771. **Merian, Mme. M. S.** Histoire Generale des Insectes de Surinam et de toute l'Europe. Paris, L. C. Desnos, 1771.

1879. **McCook, H. C.** On the Architecture and Habits of the Cutting Ant of Texas (Atta fervens). *Proc. Acad. Nat. Sci. Phila.*, Feb. 11, 1879, pp. 33–40: *Ann. Mag. Nat. Hist.* (5), III, 1879, pp. 442–449.

1880. **McCook, H. C.** Note on a New Northern Cutting Ant, Atta septentrionalis. *Proc. Acad. Nat. Sci. Phila.*, 1880, pp. 359, 360, 1 fig.

1888. **McCook, H. C.** Note on the Sense of Direction in a European Ant (Formica rufa). *Ann. Mag. Nat. Hist.* (6), II, 1888, pp. 189–192.

1902. **McCook, H. C.** Tenants of an Old Farm. Philadelphia, Geo. W. Jacobs & Co., pp. 230–276, first ed. 1884.

1893. **Mœller, A.** Die Pilzgärten einiger sudamerikanischer Ameisen. Heft VI, *Schimper's Botanische Mitth. aus d. Tropen*, 1893, 127 pp. 7 pls.

1900. **Moreno, A.** Observaciones acerca de las Costumbres de las Hormigas. *Mem. Rev. Soc. Cient. Antonio Alzate*, XIV, 1900 Rev. pp. 60–62.

1881. **Morris, G. K.** A New Leaf-cutting Ant. *Amer. Natur.*, Feb. 1881, pp. 100–102.

1874. **Müller, Fritz.** The Habits of Various Insects. (Letter to Chas. Darwin.) *Nature*, June 11, 1874, pp. 102, 103.

1883. **Müller, Fritz.** [Article on Atta]. *Blumenauer Zeitung*, 1883.

1884. **Nehrling, H.** [On Atta texana]. *Zool. Garten*, XXV, 1884, p. 265.

1535. **de Oviedo y Valdez, G. F.** Historia General de las Indias. I, lib. XV, cap. 1.

1844. **Reiche, L.** Note sur les Propriétés Lumineuses de Pyrophorus, Nyctophanes, et sur le bruit fait par les Passalus; Oecodoma cephalotes. *Ann. Soc. Entom. France*, (2), II, 1844, Bull. pp. 63–67.

1894. **Sampaio de Azevedo, A. G.** Saúva ou Manhúaára. Monographia. São Paulo, 1894.

1896(a). **Schenckling-Prévot.** Ameisen als Pilzzüchter und esser. *Illustr. Wochenschr. f. Entom.*, 1 Jahrb., no. 6, 1896, pp. 89–93.

1896(b). **Schenckling-Prévot.** Die Pilzgärten der Haarameisen. *Insektenbörse*, 13 Jahrg., 1896, pp. 153, 154.

1896(c). **Schenckling-Prévot.** Die Höckerameisen und ihre Pilzgärten. *Ibid.* p. 264.

1897. **Schenckling-Prévot.** Rozites gongylophora, die Kulturpflanze der Blattschneide-Ameisen. *Illustr. Wochenschr. f. Entom.*, 2 Jahrg., 1897, pp. 56–60.

1888. **Schimper, A. F. W.** Die Wechselbeziehungen zwischen Pflanzen und Ameisen im tropischen Amerika. *Botan. Mitth. aus den Tropen*, Heft 1, 1888, 95 pp. 3 pl.

1734–1735. **Seba, Albertus.** Locupletissimi Rerum Naturalium Thesauri Accurata Descriptio 4 vol., fol., Amstelodami, 1734–1735.

1894. **Spencer, Herbert.** Origin of Classes among the "Parasol" Ants. *Nature,* LI, 1894, pp. 125, 126.

1896. **Swingle, W. T.** Fungus Gardens in the Nest of an Ant (Atta tardigrada Buckl.) near Washington. *Proc. Am. Assoc. Adv. Sci.,* 44th Meet., 1896, pp. 185, 186.

1892(a). **Tanner, J. E.** Œcodoma cephalotes. The Parasol or Leaf-cutting Ant. *Trinidad Field Nat. Club,* I, no. 3, Aug. 1892, pp. 68, 69.

1892(b). **Tanner, J. E.** Œcodoma cephalotes. Second Paper, *Ibid.,* no. 5. Dec. 1892, pp. 123, 127.

1870. **Townsend, B. R.** The Red Ant of Texas. *Amer. Entomol. and Botan.,* St. Louis, Mo., Oct. II, 1870, no. 11, pp. 324–325.

1895(a). **Urich, F. W.** Notes on Some Fungus-growing Ants in Trinidad. *Journ. Trinidad Club,* II, no. 7, 1895, pp. 175–182.

1895(b). **Urich, F. W.** Notes on the Fungus-growing and eating Habit of Sericomyrmex opacus Mayr. *Trans. Entom. Soc. London,* 1895, pp. 77, 78.

1894. **Wasmann, Erich.** Kritisches Verzeichnis der myrmekophilen und termitophilen Arthropoden. Berlin, Felix Dames, 1894.

1895. **Wasmann, Erich.** Die Ameisen- und Termitengäste von Brasilien. *Verh. k. k. Zool. Bot. Ges. Wien,* 1895, pp. 2–46.

1900. **Wasmann, Erich.** The Guests of Ants and Termites. *Entom. Record and Journ. of Variat.,* XII, 1900, 15 pp. pl. iii.

1900. **Wheeler, W. M.** A New Myrmecophile from the Mushroom-Gardens of the Texan Leaf-cutting Ant. *Amer. Natur.,* XXXIV, 1900, pp. 851–862, 6 figg.

1901. **Wheeler, W. M.** Biological Notes on Mexican Ants. *Ann. Soc. Entom. Belg.,* XLV, 1901, pp. 199–205.

1903. **Wheeler, W. M.** The Origin of Female and Worker Ants from the Eggs of Parthenogenetic Workers. *Science,* N. S., XVIII, 1903, pp. 830–833.

1905(a). **Wheeler, W. M.** The Ants of the Bahamas, with a List of the Known West Indian Species. *Bull. Amer. Mus. Nat. Hist.,* XXI, 1905, pp. 79–135, pl. vii, text-figg.

1905(b). **Wheeler, W. M.** An Annotated List of the Ants of New Jersey. *Ibid.,* pp. 371–403.

1906(a). **Wheeler, W. M.** The Queen Ant as a Psychological study. *Popul. Sci. Month.,* Apr. 1906, pp. 291–299, 7 figg. Reprinted in *Scientif. Amer.,* Suppl. no. 1603, Sept. 22, 1906, pp. 25685, 25686.

1906(b). **Wheeler, W. M.** On the Founding of Colonies by Queen Ants, with Special Reference to the Slave-making Species. *Bull. Amer. Mus. Nat. Hist.,* XXII, 1906, pp. 33–105, pls. viii–xiv, 1 text-fig.

1882. **White.** [Great Swarms of Oecodomas in the Paraná] in "Cameos from the Silver Land," II, 1882, pp. 437, 438.

1885. **Will, F.** Die Geschmacksorgane der Insekten. *Zeitschr. f. wiss. Zool.,* XLII, 1885, pp. 674–707, Taf. XXVII.

1899. **Anonymous.** Tropische Ameisen als Pilzzüchter. *Natur,* 48 Jahrg., 1899, pp. 135–137.

b. Fungus-growing Termites.

1905. **Doflein, F.** Die Pilzkulturen der Termiten. *Verh. deutsch. zool. Ges.,* 15. Vers. pp. 140–149, 2 figg.

1906. **Doflein, F.** Ostasienfahrt. Erlebnisse und Beobachtungen eines Naturforschers in China, Japan und Ceylon. B. G. Teubner, Berlin, 1906, pp. 454–473, figg.

1900. **Errington de la Croix, Mme.** Observations sur le Termes carbonarius Haviland. *Bull. Mus. Hist. Nat. Paris*, 1900, pp. 22, 23, 1 fig.

1855–1860. **Hagen, H.** Monographie der Termiten. *Linn. Entomol.*, X, 1855, pp. 1–144, 270–325; XII, 1858, pp. 1–342, Taf. i–iii; XIV, 1860, pp. 73–128.

1907. **Harris, J. A.** The Fungi of Termite Nests. *Amer. Natur.*, XLI, 1907, pp. 536–539.

1898. **Haviland, G. D.** Observations on Termites, or White Ants. *Journ. Linn. Soc. Zool.*, XXVI, 1898, pp. 358–442, pl. xxii–xxv, 2 text-figg.; reprinted in *Ann. Rep. Smithson. Instit.*, 1901, pp. 667–678, 4 pls.

1899. **Holtermann, Carl.** Pilzbauende Termiten. *Botan. Untersuch.* (Festschr. f. Schwendener), 1899 pp. 411–420, 1 fig.

1901. **Karawaiew W.** Supplement to the Preliminary Account of an Excursion to the Island of Java. (In Russian.) *Mém. Soc. Natural. Kiew*, XVII, Livr. 1, 1901, pp. 298–303, 1 pl.

1899. **Knuth, Paul.** Termiten und ihre Pilzgärten. *Illustr. Zeitschr. f. Entom.*, IV, 1899, pp. 257–259, 4 figg.

1779. **König J. G.** Naturgeschichte der sogenannten weissen Ameise. *Beschäft. Berl. Ges. naturforsch. Freunde*, IV, 1779, pp. 1–28, Taf. i.

1906. **Petch, T.** The Fungi of Certain Termite Nests. (Termes redemanni Wasm.; and T. obscuriceps Wasm.) *Ann. Roy. Bot. Gard. Peradeniya*, III, 1906, pp. 185–270, Pl. V–XXI.

1903. **Silvestri, F.** Contribuzione alla Conoscenza dei Termitidi e Termitofili. *Redia*, I, 1903, pp. 1–234, Taf. i–vi, 57 text-figg.

1896. **Sjöstedt, Y.** Termes lilljeborgi, eine neue wahrscheinlich pilzanbauende Tagtermite aus Kamerun. Festschr. f. W. Lilljeborg. 1896, pp. 267–280, 1 Taf.

1900. **Sjöstedt, Y.** Monographie der Termiten Afrikas. *Kongl. Svenska Vetensk. Akad. Handl.*, XXXIV, no. 4, Apr. 11, 1900, 236 pp. 9 pl.

1903. **Sjöstedt, Y.** Termiterna och deras Biologi. *Ibid.*, Årsbok, 1903, pp. 89–101.

1904. **Sjöstedt, Y.** Monographie der Termiten Afrikas. Nachtrag. *Ibid.*, XXXVIII, no. 4, 1904, pp. 1–120, 4 pl.

1781. **Smeathman, Henry.** Of the Termites in Africa and Other Hot Climates. *Phil. Trans. Roy. Soc. London*, LXXI, 1781, pp. 60–85, 2 pl.

1896. **Smith, E. F.** White Ants as Cultivators of Fungi. *Amer. Natur.*, XXX, 1896, pp. 319–321.

1904. **Trägårdh, I.** Termiten aus dem Sudan. Results Swed. Zool. Exped. to Egypt and the White Nile (1901), Pt. I, 1904, pp. 1–47, 3 pl. 8 text-figg.

c. Ambrosia Beetles.

1872–1875. **Altum, B.** Forstzoologie. Berlin, 1872–1875.

1873. **Beling.** Beitrag zur Naturgeschichte des Bostrychus lineatus und des Bostrychus domesticus. *Tharander Jahrb.* XXXIII, 1873, pp. 17–44.

1899. **Eggers, H.** Zur Lebensweise des Xyleborus cryptographus Ratz. *Illustr. Zeitschr. f. Entom.*, IV, 1899, pp. 291–292, fig.

1881. **Eichhoff, W.**   Die Europäischen Borkenkäfer. Berlin, J. Springer, 1881, pp. 280–281.

1906. **Felt, E. P.**   Insects Affecting Park and Woodland Trees. N. Y. State Museum, Mem. 8, Albany, N. Y. 1906.   pp. 369–396.

1895. **Göthe, R.**   Bericht d. k. Lehranst. f. Obst-, Wein-u. Gartenbau zu Geisenheim (1894–95), 1895, p. 25.

1907. **Hagedorn.**   Pilzzüchtende Borkenkäfer. *Naturwiss. Wochenschr.*, *Neue Folge*, 6. Bd. No. 19. 12 Mai, 1907, pp. 289–293, 12 figg.

1844. **Hartig, T.**   Allgem. Forst-u. Jagtzeitg. B. XIII, 1844, pp. 73, 74.

1872a. **Hartig, T.**   Der Fichtensplintkäfer Bostrichus (Xyloterus) lineatus. *Ibid.*, XLVIII, 1872, pp. 181–183.

1872b. **Hartig, T.**   Der Buchensplintkäfer Bostrichus (Xyloterus) domesticus. *Ibid.*, XLVIII, 1872, pp. 183–184.

1906. **Hedgcock, G. G.**   Studies upon Some Chromogenic Fungi which Discolor Wood. *Seventeenth Ann. Rep. Missouri Bot. Garden*, 1906, pp. 59–114, pls. iii–xii.

1898. **Hopkins, A. D.**   On the History and Habits of the "Wood Engraver" Ambrosia Beetle — Xyleborus xylographus (Say), Xyleborus saxeseni (Ratz.) — with Brief Descriptions of Different Stages. *Canad. Entom.*, XXX, 1898, pp. 21–29, 2 pls.

1899. **Hopkins, A. D.**   Report on Investigations to Determine the Cause of Unhealthy Conditions of the Spruce and Pine from 1880–1893. *Bull. 56 West Virginia Agric. Exper. Sta.*, April, 1899.

1904(a). **Hopkins, A. D.**   Insect Injuries to Hardwood Forest Trees. Yearbook U. S. Depart. Agric. 1903, Washington, 1904, pp. 313–328, pl. xxxix, 17 text-figg.

1904(b). **Hopkins, A. D.**   Catalogue of Exhibits of Insect Enemies of Forests and Forest Products at the Louisiana Purchase Exposition. St. Louis, Mo., 1904, Washington, 1904, pp. 15, 16.

1905. **Hopkins, A. D.**   Insect Injuries to Forest Products. Year-book U. S. Dep. Agric. 1904, Washington, 1905, pp. 381–398, 14 figg.

1897(a). **Hubbard, H. G.**   The Ambrosia Beetles of the United States. *Bull. no. 7, n. s. Dep. Agric. Div. Entom.* 1897, pp. 11–30, 34 figg.

1897(b). **Hubbard, H. G.**   Ambrosia Beetles. Yearbook U. S. Dep. Agric. 1906, pp. 421–430, Washington, 1897, 7 figg.

1906. **Leisewitz, W.**   Ueber chitinöse Fortbewegungs Apparate einiger (insbesondere fussloser) Insektenlarven. München, E. Reinhardt, 1906, 143 pp. 46 figg.

1839–1844. **Ratzeburg, J. T.**   Die Forstinsekten. 3 vol., Berlin, Nicolai'sche Buchhandl., 1839–1844.

1895. **Ratzeburg, J. T.**   Lehrbuch der Mitteleuropäischen Forstinsektenkunde. 8 Aufl. Vienna, Ed. Hölzel, Bd. I, 1895.

1836. **Schmidberger.**   Beiträge zur Obstbaumzucht und zur Naturgeschichte der den Obstbäumen schädlichen Insecten. Heft. IV, Linz, 1836.

1903. **von Schrenk, H.**   The "Bluing" and the "Red Rot" of the Western Yellow Pine, with Special Reference to the Black Hills Forest Reserve, U. S. Dep. Agric. Bur. Plant Indust. Bull. No. 26. Washington, 1903, 40 pp. 14 pll.

1896. **Smith, E. T.**   Ambrosia. *Amer. Nat.*, XXX, 1896, pp. 318, 319.

PLATES

EXPLANATION OF THE PLATES.

PLATE XLIX.

Fig. 1.— *Cyphomyrmex rimosus* Spinola var. *comalensis* var. nov.   Worker.
Fig. 2.— *Cyphomyrmex wheeleri* Forel.   Worker.
Fig. 3.— *Atta (Trachymyrmex) turrifex* Wheeler.   Worker.
Fig. 4.— *Atta (Trachymyrmex) septentrionalis* McCook.   Worker.
Fig. 5.— *Atta (Mœllerius) versicolor* Pergande.   Worker.
Fig. 6.— *Atta (Mycetosoritis) hartmanni* sp. nov.   Worker.
Fig. 7.— The same in profile.
Fig. 8.— *A. (M.) hartmanni* sp. nov.   Male.
Fig. 9.— *Atta (Trachymyrmex) arizonensis* sp. nov.   Deälated female in profile.
Fig. 10.— Head of same from above.
Fig. 11.— *Atta texana* Buckley.   Soldier.
Fig. 12.— Thorax of same in profile.
Fig. 13.— *Atta texana*.   Media.
Fig. 14.— *Atta texana*.   Minima.

PLATE XLIX.

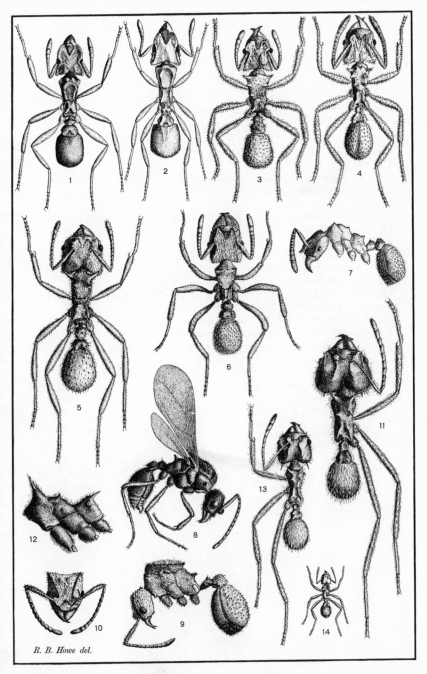

R. B. Howe del.

PLATE L.

Fig. 15.— *Atta* (*Mycocepurus*) *smithi* Forel.   Worker.

Fig. 16.— Same in profile.

Fig. 17.— *Sericomyrmex opacus* Mayr.   Worker.

Fig. 18.— *Myrmicocrypta brittoni* sp. nov.   Worker.

Fig. 19.— Same in profile.

Fig. 20.— *Apterostigma pilosum* Mayr.   Worker.

Fig. 21.   *Atta sexdens* L. Brazil.   Hypopygium of male.

Fig. 22.— *Atta cephalotes* L. Panama.   Hypopygium of male.

Fig. 23.— *Atta insularis* Guérin.   Cuba.   Hypopygium of male.

Fig. 24.— *Atta texana* Buckley.   Texas.   Hypopygium of male.

Fig. 25.— *Atta mexicana* F. Smith.   Mexico.   Hypopygium of male.

Fig. 26.— *Atta* (*Mœllerius*) *versicolor* Pergande.   Male.   Genitalia from above.

Fig. 27.— Unusual triple nest-entrance of *Trachymyrmex turrifex*.

Fig. 28.— Unusual double nest-entrance of *Mycetosoritis hartmanni*.

Fig. 29.— Bromatia of fungus (*Tyridiomyces formicarum* gen. et sp. nov.), cultivated and eaten by *Cyphomyrmex rimosus* and its various subspecies and varieties.

PLATE L.

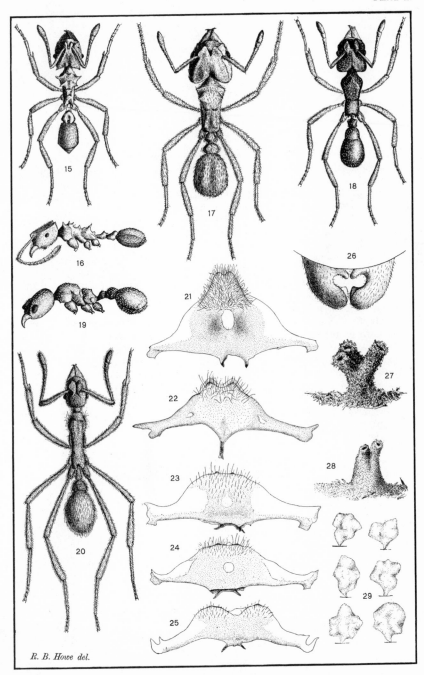

R. B. Howe del.

PLATE LI.

Fig. 30.— Nest diagram of *Mycetosoritis hartmanni* (Nest X of the table on p. 763), showing four chambers, the connecting galleries, and the pendent fungus gardens.

Fig. 31.— Nest diagram of *M. hartmanni* (Nest T of the table on p. 763), with three chambers all containing fungus gardens.

Fig. 32.— Nest diagram of *M. hartmanni* (Nest U of the table on p. 763), with three chambers.

Fig. 33.— Nest diagram of *Trachymyrmex turrifex* (Nest L of the diagram on p. 756), with five well-developed chambers and pendent fungus gardens in all but the first.

Fig. 34.— Nest diagram of *T. turrifex* (Nest N of the table on p. 756), with four chambers, the lowermost small, recently excavated, and with an incipient garden suspended from rootlets.

Fig. 35.— Nest diagram of *T. turrifex* (Nest O of the table on p. 756), with four well-developed chambers and flourishing gardens in three of them.

Fig. 36.— Nest diagram of *T. turrifex* (Nest P of the table on p. 756), with five chambers and poorly developed fungus gardens in three of them. This nest shows very clearly the suspension of the substratum from the rootlets hanging into or traversing the chambers.

Fig. 37.— Nest diagram of *Trachymyrmex septentrionalis* var. *obscurior* (Nest C of the table on p. 749), consisting of only two chambers, both containing pendent fungus gardens.

Fig. 38.— Nest diagram of *T. obscurior* (Nest D of the table on p. 749), consisting of three chambers two of which open directly into each other. The mound of sand is shown in the typical position in front of the oblique entrance gallery. The first chamber contains exhausted substratum ready to be carried out of the nest.

PLATE LI.

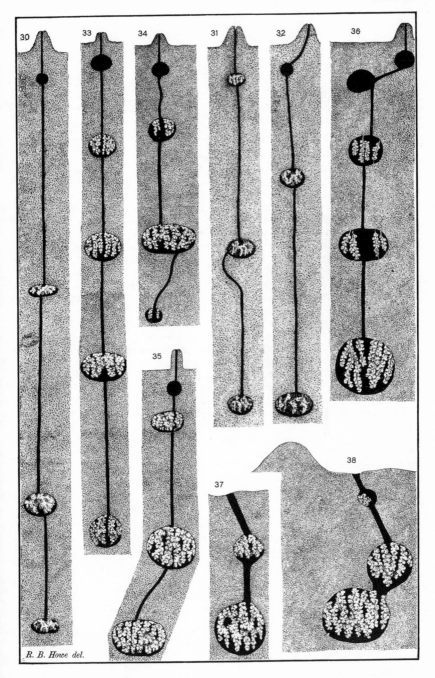

R. B. Howe del.

PLATE LII.

Fig. 39.— Nest diagram of *Trachymyrmex obscurior* (Nest I of the table on p. 749), of the racemose type, with five chambers. Extending from the single chamber on the right is an unfinished gallery. All the chambers contain well-developed pendent gardens except the first, which is partially filled with exhausted substratum.

Fig. 40.— Nest diagram of *T. obscurior* (Nest J of the table on p. 749) of the racemose type, with seven chambers, six of which are of large size. Of the latter, five contain flourishing gardens but one (to the extreme right) seems to have been only recently excavated by the ants. The crater of this nest was best developed behind the entrance.

Fig. 41.— Nest diagram of *T. obscurior* (Nest G of the table on p. 749) of the racemose and horizontally spreading type, with four chambers. The first chamber, in which the mother queen established her colony, had been subsequently enlarged by the workers.

Fig. 42.— Nest diagram of *T. obscurior* (Nest H of the table on p. 749) of the racemose type, with four chambers. As in the preceding, the first chamber had been enlarged by the workers, the lowermost was apparently in process of excavation.

Fig. 43.— Cells composing the bromatia of *Tyridiomyces formicarum*, the peculiar fungus grown by *Cyphomyrmex rimosus*.

Fig. 44.— Cells composing the bromatia of the same or an allied species of *Tyridiomyces* grown by *Mycocepurus smithi* var. *borinquenensis*.

PLATE LII.

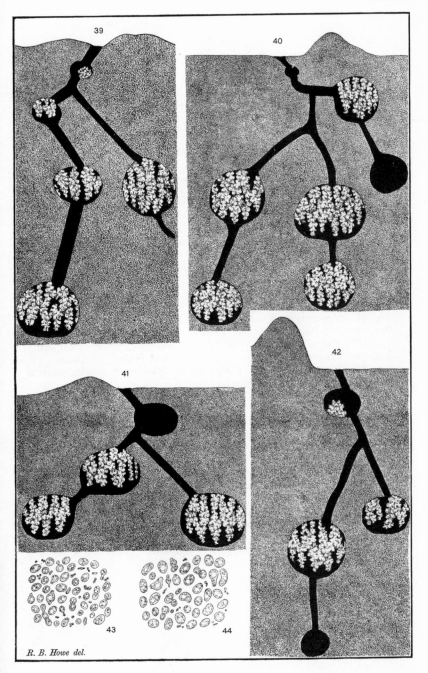

R. B. Howe del.

PLATE LIII.

Fig. 45.— Nest diagram of *Trachymyrmex obscurior* (Nest F of the table on p. 749), resembling the nests of *T. turrifex*, with five chambers.

Fig. 46.— Nest diagram of *Trachymyrmex turrifex* (Nest R of the table on p. 756) in pure sand, showing the elongation of the galleries.

Fig. 46a.— Deeper portion of the same nest with incipient gardens on the rootlets traversing the two lower chambers.

Fig. 47.— *Attaphila fungicola* Wheeler. Male. From nest of *Atta texana*.

Fig. 48.— *A. fungicola.* Female; dorsal view.

Fig. 49.— Same, ventral view.

Fig. 50.— *Attaphila bergi* Bolivar. Male, from nest of *Acromyrmyx lundi.* (After Bolivar.)

Fig. 51.— *A. bergi,* Female. (After Bolivar.)

Fig. 52.— Head of same. (After Bolivar.)

Fig. 53.— Hypopygium of same. (After Bolivar.)

Fig. 54.— *A. bergi.*— Hypopygium of male. (After Bolivar.)

Fig. 55.— Fungus garden of *Termes bellicosus* Smeathm. (After Smeathman.)

Fig. 56.— Bromatia of same more highly magnified. (After Smeathman.)

Fig. 57.— Portion of the fungus garden of a Malayan *Termes*, showing spherical bromatia of *Agaricus rajap* Holtermann. (After Karawaiew.) Natural size.

Fig. 58.— Bromatium from the fungus garden of an African Termite, *Termes vulgaris* Havil. (After Trägårdh.)

Fig. 59.— Portion of same crushed under a cover-glass and more highly magnified, to show the component cells. (After Trägårdh.)

Fig. 60.— A fungus garden of the African *Eutermes heterodon* Sjöst. $\frac{2}{3}$ natural size. (After Sjöstedt.)

Fig. 61.— Section of same. (After Sjöstedt.)

Fig. 62.— Ambrosia beetle (*Xyleborus celsus* Eichh.) of the hickory. Female, enlarged. (After Hubbard.)

Fig. 63.— *X. celsus,* Male. (After Hubbard.)

Fig. 64.— Piece of hickory showing burrows of *X. celsus* in the sapwood. (After Hopkins.)

Fig. 65.— "Ambrosia" or fungus grown by *X. celsus* enlarged. On the right a few of the filaments more highly magnified.

PLATE LIII.

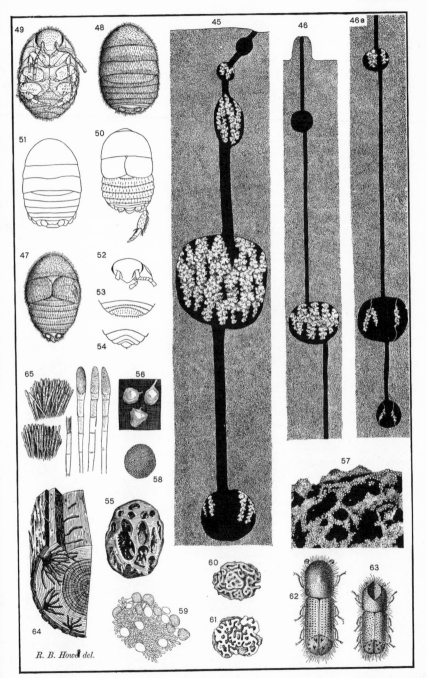

R. B. Howell del.